Good Business

Also by Mihaly Csikszentmihalyi

Good Work
When Excellence and Ethics Meet
(coauthored with Howard Gardner and William Damon)

Finding Flow
The Psychology of Engagement with Everyday Life

Creativity
Flow and the Psychology of Discovery and Invention

The Evolving Self
A Psychology for the Third Millennium

Flow
The Psychology of Optimal Experience

Good Business

Leadership, Flow, and the Making of Meaning

Mihaly Csikszentmihalyi

VIKING

VIKING
Published by the Penguin Group
Penguin Putnam Inc., 375 Hudson Street, New York, New York 10014, U.S.A.
Penguin Books Ltd, 80 Strand, London WC2R 0RL, England
Penguin Books Australia Ltd, 250 Camberwell Road, Camberwell, Victoria 3124, Australia
Penguin Books Canada Ltd, 10 Alcorn Avenue, Toronto, Ontario, Canada M4V 3B2
Penguin Books India (P) Ltd, 11 Community Centre, Panchsheel Park, New Delhi -
110 017, India
Penguin Books (N.Z.) Ltd, Cnr Rosedale and Airborne Roads, Albany, Auckland,
New Zealand
Penguin Books (South Africa) (Pty) Ltd, 24 Sturdee Avenue, Rosebank, Johannesburg
2196, South Africa

Penguin Books Ltd, Registered Offices: Harmondsworth, Middlesex, England

First published in 2003 by Viking Penguin, a member of Penguin Putnam Inc.

10   9   8   7   6   5   4   3   2   1

CIP data available

ISBN 0-670-03196-8

This book is printed on acid-free paper. ∞

Printed in the United States of America
Set in New Baskerville
Designed by Nancy Resnick

Acknowledgments

If I were to mention all the people whose ideas and inspiration have made this book possible, it would add the equivalent of another chapter to its length. So I'll have to be selective and list only the names of those people whose contributions have been absolutely indispensable. First among these are the visionary leaders whose interviews provide the many quotations in the pages that follow—their names are listed in the first endnote. Their wisdom and experience have added a great deal of insight to this book.

I shared the design and the conduct of the study on which the book is based with my friends and colleagues Howard Gardner from Harvard University and William Damon from Stanford. Their enduring friendship has been a wonderful complement to the intellectual work we have done together over the years. My young colleagues at the Quality of Life Research Center, Jeanne Nakamura and Jeremy Hunter, have helped immeasurably both with collecting the interviews and with their continuing stimulation and support. The Good Work in Business study itself was made possible by a grant from the Templeton Foundation. Besides Sir John Templeton himself, I would like to thank Arthur Schwartz, who acted as program officer. As usual, their generosity matched their discretion—no strings were attached to the grant, and I can only hope that our results will not disappoint them.

The president of the Claremont Graduate University, Steadman

Upham, and the dean of the School of Management, Cornelius de Kluyver, have followed this work from its beginning and been its vigorous advocates. Of the many colleagues at Claremont from whose knowledge and experience I have benefited I should single out first Peter Drucker and then Jeanne Lippman-Blumen, Richard Ellsworth, and Joseph Maciariello. My thanks also go to the students in the executive management program who took my courses and who have read early drafts of this book and have commented on them. Their experience in the trenches made me confident that the issues I was tackling were important and meaningful to a great variety of businesspeople. Loren Bryant did a superb job making sure that the manuscript was in good shape and all the permissions secured.

At the University of Chicago, Barbara Schneider has continued to assist with her collegial collaboration, and so did Martin Seligman from the University of Pennsylvania. I am grateful for the friendship of many colleagues in Europe—Fausto Massimini and Antonella delle Fave from Milan, Paolo Inghilleri from Verona, Elizabeth Noelle-Neumann from Allensbach, George Klein from Stockholm, among others.

Rick Kot, my once and future editor, has again helped to focus the paragraphs into streamlined, literate prose. John Brockman and Katinka Matson, who have been agents for my books for the past decade and a half, again made sure that the manuscript would find a good home in a publishing house. It is a huge relief to be assisted by the advice of such professionals as these three are.

And finally, I am deeply grateful to my family—above all, to my wife, Isabella, then to Mark and his wonderful family, and to Christopher. Without their loving support, this book would certainly not have been written.

Claremont, 2003

Contents

Part I

Flow and Happiness

Chapter 1

Leading the Future

Our jobs determine to a large extent what our lives are like. Is what you do for a living making you ill? Does it keep you from becoming a more fully realized person? Do you feel ashamed of what you have to do at work? All too often, the answer to such questions is yes. Yet it does not have to be like that. Work can be one of the most joyful, most fulfilling aspects of life. Whether it will be or not depends on the actions we collectively take. If the firms that employ an increasing majority of the population are driven solely to satisfy the owners' greed at the expense of working conditions, of the stability of the community, and of the health of the environment, chances are that the quality of our lives—and that of our children—will be worse than it is now.

Fortunately, despite the scandals that have rocked the business world at the start of this century, there are still corporate leaders who understand that they are allowed to hold their privileges only because the rest of us expect them to improve the conditions of existence, rather than help to destroy them. This book is a survey of some of their values, their goals, their mode of operation—a guidebook for a way of conducting business that is both successful and humane.

While the book draws primarily on the experience of leaders of major corporations, it is really about how to improve one's work life at any level—be it janitor or manager. It tries to provide a context for a meaningful life in which work and the pursuit of financial rewards can find their proper places. The men and women we interviewed* had been nominated by their peers because they were both successful and because they cared for more than success. In one way or another, they all had demonstrated that selfish advantage was not their sole motivation. Their collective wisdom provides a blueprint for doing business that is good in both senses: the material and the spiritual.

Now that the entire nation is finally calling the bluff of rogue CEOs, every business leader is eager to mouth pieties to camouflage his true priorities. After the corporate giant Enron collapsed and became a global byword for irresponsible management, one of its leading executives, Jeff Skilling, described his job as doing "God's work." His CEO, Kenneth Lay, had earlier declared: "I was, and am, a strong believer that one of the most satisfying things in life is to create a highly moral and ethical environment in which every individual is allowed and encouraged to realize that God-given potential."

These are worthy sentiments, but worse than useless if one's actions do not support them. As opposed to those leaders who use language only as a disguise, the people on whose experience this book is based actually have shown that they tried hard to create ethical environments in which individuals could realize their potentials. By no means did they always live up to their stated intentions; but their ideas, words, and example show that doing business can be much more fulfilling than most of us realize. So, based in large part on the experience of these exemplary CEOs, this book will discuss what it means to be a good leader, a good manager, and a good worker.

Bookstores are full of volumes containing very good advice about how to be an effective manager or successful leader. Often such

---

*See note 1, p. 213.

books will instruct a reader to model his or her behavior on the cynical wisdom of Machiavelli, the relentless drive of Genghis Khan, or the ruthlessness of Attila the Hun as a way to achieve power and plunder. *Good Business* has a more modest ambition. It will explore how leaders who have impressed their peers for both their *business success* and their *commitment to broader social goals* go about their jobs—what ambitions motivate them, and what kind of organizations they try to develop in pursuit of those ideals.

The necessity for considering such issues is simple: Today business leaders are among the most influential members of society. While they are all trained to generate profits, many of them are oblivious to the other responsibilities that their new societal leadership entails. In this book, visionary leaders will explain what they consider to be their duties and how they go about fulfilling them. In the process of examining their philosophies and their practical applications, we will focus especially on how leaders and managers and even the concerned employees of any organization can learn to contribute to the sum of human happiness, to the development of an enjoyable life that provides meaning, and to a society that is just and evolving.

These may seem like goals that are beyond human reach, and certainly outside the scope of a book dealing with business. But the way we make a living, the jobs we have, and the way our work is rewarded have a tremendous bearing on our lives, making them either exciting and rewarding, or dull and anxious. For that reason alone anyone in charge of a workplace is obliged to consider the question: How am I contributing to human well-being? This is certainly not a concern that motivated Genghis Khan, or even Machiavelli. But to follow the examples of such social predators prevents business leaders from achieving their full potential. Of course there will always be single-mindedly ambitious executives concerned only with clawing their way to the top. But is such behavior really the kind of leadership we want in our society? In fact, there are enough people in business who do genuinely value organizations that promote happiness, and it is my hope that this book will help them.

As a first step, we should consider what it has meant to be a successful leader in the past, so that we can understand better what options the future may hold.

As humans, we cannot survive without hope. When we lack reasons for living apart from the urges that biology has built into our nervous system we soon revert to an animal level of existence, where only food, comfort, and sex matter. By contrast, the remarkable cultures that some of the great world civilizations have occasionally achieved were made possible by two very different prerequisites: a reasonable level of resources and the technology to use them, leading to a material surplus; and a defined set of goals that helped their citizens overcome the inevitable obstacles and tragedies inherent in living. If either of these conditions is absent, life devolves to a selfish scramble; if both are lacking, it becomes utterly hopeless.

Depending on the level of societal development, a particular class of individuals may step forth with the promise of improving the material conditions of the populace, and offer a set of goals for channeling its life energy. If these individuals can make a credible claim for their program, they are likely to emerge as the leaders of society because the rest of the population will agree to follow them. For untold thousands of years these leaders were typically the best hunters of the tribe, who offered good spoils to their followers, and inspiring stories about the happy hunting grounds in the thereafter. As technologies of food production and warfare became more advanced, however, groups of warlords and of kings surrounded by courtiers and priests assumed leadership. In some periods the clergy and the nobility—usually made up of great landowners—jointly shared power. More recently merchants and manufacturers have risen to the top of the social pyramid.

At the present time two categories of individuals hold the clearest title to providing for the material and spiritual needs of the community. The first is scientists, who promise hope through a longer and healthier life, an expansion of our ambitions into the solar system, and eventual control over both animate and inanimate matter. The second and larger group consists of men and women engaged in business, who promise to make our lives more affluent, comfortable, and exciting by allowing market forces to direct production and consumption in the most efficient way. Scientists and business leaders—the elite of the new knowledge workforce—have achieved an eminence reserved in former times for the nobility and the clergy. Those who do not belong to their ranks are nevertheless willing to grant them power and wealth because they believe that society as a whole will ultimately benefit from their efforts. Is this faith misplaced?

It is difficult to answer that question objectively, let alone accurately. But I believe that most people would agree that science (along with its handmaiden, technology) and business have indeed created living conditions that are more desirable than any that ever existed. Let us set aside for a moment the very real issue of whether such material blessings can be sustained indefinitely, or even as long as into the coming decades. Huge problems confront us, ranging from the inevitable depletion of scarce natural resources, to the many stresses of our increasingly hard-driven lifestyles, to the strains resulting from the unequal allocation of resources among the rich and the poor both within and between societies. Let us also overlook the real costs of progress in terms of maladies like drug addiction, violence, and depression, which have become so endemic in technologically advanced societies, and concede the fact that scientific and entrepreneurial leadership has indeed delivered on the promise of a more desirable material existence.

That leaves, however, the second condition for a good life unaccounted for. What about the sense of hope that successful leaders are also supposed to convey to those who follow them? In this area, the results are more equivocal. Basically science and business both follow empirical, pragmatic, value-free methods. Although there are individual scientists and business leaders who take a quasi-religious stance toward their work, they usually do so by drawing on some established spiritual or moral tradition, and not on any particular tenets of their profession. Science can promise truth, but its version of truth is as often harsh as it is soothing. Business promises efficiency and profit, but what do these achievements contribute toward filling life with joy and meaning?

Most leaders of business and science would argue that it is not their responsibility to cater to the spiritual needs of society, a job that is better left to the clergy, or even political leaders. But for many people, traditional religions and political parties seem to have run out of visions compelling enough to provide global leadership. If no one else steps forward to assume that role we risk succumbing to charlatans and demagogues—a fate that has befallen many powerful and rich societies.

It is useful to reflect on the patterns of history so that we may learn from them and avoid having to repeat the mistakes of our ancestors. In the past a leading elite has usually emerged because it promised to improve the life of the majority. At that point at least some of the energy of its leaders was directed outward, working for the benefit of others. For instance the early Christian Church helped the downtrodden multitudes of the Roman Empire to find meaning and dignity in their existence. This very success resulted, however, in the church's being populated by ever greater numbers of clergy attracted primarily by a selfish desire for comfort and power, so that increasingly it withdrew its energies from the community and used them instead for its own profit. While the hovels of medieval peasants remained dark and dirty century after century, the palaces of the princes of the church became ever more resplendent. Eventually leaders with credible messages of hope had to separate themselves from the hierarchy of the Church; first from within it, as spiritual innovators like Saint Bernard or Saint Francis did, and later in opposition to it, like Luther and Calvin.

Similar cycles of hope and disillusion have recurred in most societies around the world. Lord Asquith, premier of Great Britain, once said that "All civilizations are the work of aristocracies"—to which Winston Churchill retorted: "It is more accurate to say that aristocracies are what civilizations have had to work for." Both aphorisms are valid, although they refer to different phases of the cycle—Asquith describing the brief dawn, and Churchill the much longer period that follows.

The parallels with our own times are quite obvious. For the past century or so, business leaders have made credible claims to the effect that allowing for the operation of a free market, unfettered by social and political regulations, would improve the quality of life for everyone. As a result, our mental model of how the world works has become one in which production and consumption, the twin poles of economics, are the benchmarks of prosperity and well-being. Any fraction of a percent drop in consumption becomes a flag of distress that sends investors scurrying for shelter. After the terrorist attack of September 11, 2001, one of the most often heard responses from political and business leaders was: "Go out and buy. Don't let the enemy threaten your way of life." While this worldview offers an easy solution, and is convenient for those who benefit from it at the higher levels of the supply hierarchy, is a way of life that has consumption as its highest aim really that rewarding?

For much of the last century, the message of capitalism was opposed by what to many seemed to be the equally powerful vision of socialist states, in which centrally prioritized needs dictated production and consumption. The socialist solution, however, turned out to have feet of clay. It collapsed in part because it could not produce the promised material benefits, and in part because its political organization turned out to be even more vulnerable to the greed of its leaders than Church hierarchies, aristocracies, or mercantile elites had been.

The capitalist vision now stands alone on the world stage. Will those who promote it understand and accept the responsibilities that come with the privileges they have been given? Or will they, like so many leading classes before them, believe that their power was fairly won, that they owe nothing to the less fortunate whose toil funds their bonuses and stock options?

It would be easy to take a cynical perspective and conclude that human nature being what it is, greed will invariably prevail, and today's financial leaders will keep accumulating wealth until either the internal discrepancies in income become too blatant for the social fabric to withstand, or until a global desperation proves that Karl Marx was actually right (even though he could not foresee a truly international proletariat lashing out against the capitalist nations, who have now taken up the role that the capitalist classes once occupied within nations in the nineteenth century). Yet however dispiriting the historical record may seem to be, human nature is not, in fact, based on greed alone. In every historical period there have been individuals who care for more than their own profit, who find fulfillment in dedicating themselves to the advancement of the common good. The struggle between selfishness and altruism has run throughout history like periods of sunlight and shade on a summer afternoon.

Many business leaders today do view their jobs as entailing responsibility for the welfare of the wider community. These individuals do not define themselves as profit-making machines whose only reason for existing is to satisfy escalating expectation for immediate gain. It is to such visionary leaders that my colleagues and I turned, to learn what lessons they may have for others involved in business, as well as for everyone else who lives in these times. What do they consider their mission to be? What do they do to make life better for themselves and for others? Is there hope for society as a whole in the example they provide?

The Hundred-Year Managers

Recently I had a meeting with Yvon Chouinard, the founder of Patagonia, the manufacturer of outdoor gear. His office was located in a stucco building painted in pastel colors, hidden among eucalyptus and jacaranda trees in a quiet cul-de-sac. Inside the spaces were simple and serene with old hardwoods, glass, and ferns hanging from exposed beams. Employees in shorts and sandals moved around the premises as comfortably as if they were walking from the kitchen to the bedroom of their own homes. Sunshine shimmered through strands of wisteria, and the ocean stretched peacefully one block to the west, bearing the Channel Islands on the horizon. Occasionally the laughter of small children erupted from the day-care center on the floor below. I complimented Chouinard on how handsome an environment he had managed to carve out of an abandoned industrial building that was almost a century old.

"Yeah," he answered, "you don't build something like this if you're going to go public in three years and cash out and walk away. So we really do try to act like this company is going to be here a hundred years from now."

Chouinard's program speaks to a fundamental aspect of human nature: We need a certain amount of stability in our lives. But it is not enough simply to know that the sun is going to rise the next morning, and that the robins will return in the spring. We also have to feel that despite chaos and entropy, there is some order and permanence in our relationships and that our lives are not wasted, and will leave some trace in the sands of time. In short, we must have the conviction that our existence serves a useful purpose and has value. In the past the family provided focus to day-to-day life. Then, for several centuries, the Church assumed that role, as did local communities, who took care of their own. In more recent times a remarkable individual business—a factory, a bank, a proud old store—stood as a beacon of enlightenment and social responsibility. Today, business leaders cannot begin to foster a climate of positive order if their sole concern is making a profit. They must also have a vision that gives life meaning, that offers people hope for their own future and those of their children. We have learned how to develop five-minute and even one-minute managers. But we would do better to ask ourselves what it takes to be an executive who helps build a better future. More than anything else, we need *hundred-year managers* at the helm of corporations.

Halfway around the world, in an elegant apartment in Milan, a few steps from La Scala, Enrico Randone discusses his career. He has been working for the Italian insurer Assicurazioni Generali since he was a teenager, an orphan who had to support a mother and several brothers and sisters. Now eighty years old, he has been president and chairman of the board since he was sixty-nine—the youngest man to hold these positions in the 250 years of the company's history. If you stand in the Piazza Venezia of Rome, one of the main squares of the city, looking up at the balcony from which Mussolini used to threaten the world, the palazzo of the Assicurazioni Generali would be at your back. In Venice it faces St. Mark's Cathedral, and in almost every other Italian city the offices of the insurance company are located in an ancient palace, at the center of town. "Every policy we issue is backed by gold or real estate" says Randone of the firm that he reveres more than the Church, more than the government, more than any other earthly institution. "It is an awesome trust that every one of our twenty thousand employees is proud to be a part of."

In today's world it is primarily businesses that have the power and the responsibility to make our lives comfortable and secure. But how many firms are actually taking up this challenge? How many MBAs are taught that a "bottom line" based solely on finances is a tragic simplification? As companies dissolve and morph into new shapes, shedding employees and commitments in the process, it would seem that fewer and fewer individuals take such responsibilities seriously. But there are some executives who don't view their calling as managing merely for the next five minutes, or even the next year or decade. They have, like Enrico Randore, committed themselves for a lifetime, and beyond. In many ways, our very future depends on such visionaries.

Yvon Chouinard began his professional career as an itinerant blacksmith smitten by a love for the mountains. He spent every

day he could among the dizzying spires of the Sierras, systemati-
cally climbing their most exposed routes. He became a legend
among climbers. In the euphoric 1960s, sleeping on the shores of
mountain lakes and trying out new passages up the polished rock
walls of Yosemite seemed a good enough way to live, even though
he couldn't earn a cent doing it. Chouinard describes this period:

> I had no idea what I wanted to do in life. I started out as
> a craftsman. And my craft was climbing mountains,
> really. And then I just happened to have a lot of interest
> in the tools of climbing. In those days, it was very diffi-
> cult to buy European climbing equipment. . . . So I
> decided to make my own stuff.

With his metal-working skills he was able to forge better climbing hardware than what others were producing. At campgrounds
he started selling pitons and snap rings from the back of his beat-
up station wagon. In a few years he had a thriving business making
climbing gear.

But success turned out to be bittersweet: As the sport of climbing grew popular, the majestic rock faces became pitted and scarred
from the hardware hammered into them. Some people would have
regarded this as the inevitable price of progress and forged ahead.
But when Chouinard realized he was helping to ruin the mountains he loved, he knew he couldn't live with himself unless he
changed course. So he invented a new way of climbing with gear
that could be placed into already-existing cracks and removed
easily afterward, thus keeping the mountains clean. Eventually he
eased out of hardware altogether and started making clothes—but
clothes that were so durable that a blacksmith would be satisfied
with them.

> The first pair of shorts, we had to sew it on a machine
> for sewing leather. I used a very heavy canvas. In fact,
> the woman who sewed them stood them up, and they

stood up on the table. And that was the birth of our Standup Short. We were blacksmiths making clothes.

But switching from hardware to clothing did not change what the company stood for: "We have a philosophy of trying to have every single product we make be the best in the world," says Chouinard. "Not among the best—but *the* best. Every single thing, whether it's a pair of pants or a shirt, whatever." To build an enterprise that will endure, one must believe in the value of one's work. If an enterprise does not aspire to be the best of its kind, it will attract second-rate employees, and it will be soon forgotten.

In the course of a walk on the hills overlooking Lake Constance in the south of Germany, Elisabeth Noelle-Neumann came to a point from which she could see below her the buildings of the public opinion research institute (the Allensbach Institute) that she had built around the nucleus of a four-hundred-year-old farm. She pointed to the tile roofs sheltered by trees and said: "The most important thing in my life is to make sure that the work we do there will continue after I'm gone." Elisabeth is passionate in her belief that, for a democratic government to work, the thoughts and desires of the people must be heard. Thus public opinion surveys—especially when conducted with the painstaking professionalism of her own institute—are a bulwark of freedom. She started the institute half a century ago, right after the end of World War II, with her first husband; after his death, she ran the firm by herself. Her surveys were so accurate that soon they became a powerful political tool; in the volatile postwar years she was often threatened and publicly vilified by radical mobs as a supporter of conservative causes. Although hurt and angry, Elisabeth trusted that her work was essential, and never wavered in trying to perfect the methods of her craft.

Public ownership of companies is intended to spread the bounty of capitalism widely. But the relationship of stock owners to the companies in which they invest tends to be impersonal. We seldom care about what a firm makes—whether it is cheap weapons, poisonous pesticides, or vacuous entertainment. We pay little attention to how it markets its products, or how it treats its customers, or how it affects the community where it operates. As long as it makes profits, we endorse its management. But let the CEO's performance slip one quarter, and we hasten to take our nest egg elsewhere. Not surprisingly young managers learn quickly that the quarterly report is almighty, and live in terror of its recurring shadow ever after.

At the beginning of the last century in a small town in the Midwest, about forty miles southeast of Indianapolis, a banker bought himself a horseless carriage. With it came a driver, who happened to be a clever engineer in the bargain. He convinced the banker that diesel engines had a bright future, and the two men began experimenting with them. They built a small factory, and the banker kept investing more and more of the family funds in it. For twenty years, there was no sign of profit. Then things began to pick up, and today you can see diesels made by Cummins in Columbus, Indiana, powering many of the rigs that crisscross the continent. The business has never been easy. Almost every year a new crisis—a competitor's improved product, a cash crunch, an oil embargo, new emission standards—has threatened the viability of the company. Whenever the market undervalued it and left it vulnerable to a takeover, the family bought up enough shares to protect its autonomy.

"The reason we are still doing this," explains J. Irwin Miller, a member of the third generation to run the firm, "is because we have an obligation to the community. We could have moved somewhere where labor was cheaper, but what's the point of making some more money if you have to uproot thousands of people you know and who trust you?" Each day as he walks to work, Miller passes by some of the most beautiful modern buildings in the world. His firm has made a deal with the town, agreeing to pay for the architects' fees whenever a new church, school, fire station, or jail needs to be built. Columbus is now home to a church by Eero Saarinen and a library by I. M. Pei, and architectural tours bring

thousands of visitors from New York City and from abroad to mar-
vel at the modernist icons rising from the cornfields. Although the
company has lasted almost a hundred years, how much longer can
it endure, buffeted by the rage for profits and expansion?

As any businessperson knows, a firm's survival is never guaran-
teed; year by year, month by month, a variety of hazards must be
confronted—even when profit alone is the goal. The situation becomes even more difficult when the company is dedicated to
achieving more than just financial gains. When in order to avoid
scarring the mountains Yvon Chouinard redirected Patagonia
from manufacturing climbing hardware to clothes, he relied primarily on cotton. Slowly, however, he began to realize that cotton
raised by industrial means accounts for 25 percent of the world's
pesticide use: It takes more than two gallons of oil—the base of
pesticides—to make a single cotton shirt. In the course of a visit to
one of his suppliers, he realized he had another crisis of conscience to confront:

> When I went through the Central Valley I saw these big
> ponds out there where the water seeps from the cotton
> fields. And they have guys with cannons and shotguns to
> scare the birds away, so they don't land in this soup. You
> see all that and you talk to the farmers, and you see that
> the cancer rate is ten times above normal. I said: "That's
> it! I'll never use again another piece of industrially
> grown cotton." ... It's like waking up one day and
> you're in the business of making landmines and you go
> and see what they do. Well, you have a choice: You can
> just keep right on doing it or you have to stop. And I just
> said: "That's it! We are out of the business. I'll shut this
> place down before I continue."

But with the dogged perseverance shared by all visionary leaders, Chouinard did not close his factory. Instead, he began using

organically grown cotton for his fabrics, even though it was more expensive. The demand from his firm encouraged growers to cultivate more organic cotton, and over the years an increasing number of manufacturers like Nike, Gap, and Levi Strauss followed Patagonia's example, at least in part. Organic fiber is still a small percentage of total cotton production, but its use is increasing, and its viability demonstrates that business need not follow slavishly the rule of greed and expedience when it conflicts with more important goals.

But one does not only have to be a business leader to believe in what one does, and to think long-term. It is not a luxury or prerogative of the elite. The shipping clerk or cafeteria cook who is committed to the work she is doing is more likely to get ahead and succeed. And what's more important, she will enjoy her work and feel good about herself while doing it. That, and not just profit, is the true bottom-line measure of any human activity, business included.

To take the long view may seem anachronistic when even successful firms fold on the average after thirty years—a shorter span than the career of a typical worker. And in this postindustrial, postmodern age isn't change a more valuable commodity than stability? Isn't stability a sign of a mediocre rigidity? In fact, we seldom have to worry that businesses will become rigid with age. Even with the best of intentions, most enterprises will transform, sell out, or fail. Consider the fact that of the several hundred makers of cars at the beginning of the last century, only three survived; the same fate is likely to befall the hundreds of start-ups at the frontiers of the new economy.

As Schumpeter wrote long ago, "creative destruction" is the road to productivity. He may have been right as far as creating shareholder value is concerned, but if we take a broader view of what constitutes well-being, then creative destruction must be tempered by a concern for enduring values. Besides, when "destruction" consists of gutting firms and scattering employees to the winds like useless chaff, it is not "creative" in any sense of the term—it's just an expedient tactic in the service of greed. To resist these entropic forces we need leaders who honor the long view.

The argument presented in the following chapter concerns happiness, and specifically, what business can do to increase the sum of human well-being. This is a matter that business leaders have justifiably been able to ignore as long as they were among the majority struggling against an oppressive aristocracy. But now that business has emerged as the leading segment of society, it has inherited with this power the task of answering that most basic question: Can it make people's lives happier?

As we all suspect, and as recent research has confirmed, the answer to this question cannot rely on material inducements alone. Money, security and comfort may be necessary to make us happy, but they are definitely not sufficient. A person must also feel that his or her talents are fully employed, that he is able to develop his potentialities, and that his everyday life is not stressful or boring, but holds deeply enjoyable experiences. Chapter 3 describes how flow—as I call this subjective experience of full involvement with life—can be achieved.

However, a good life consists of more than simply the totality of enjoyable experiences. It must also have a meaningful pattern, a trajectory of growth that results in the development of increasing emotional, cognitive, and social complexity. Chapter 4 describes what the steps in this development are, and begins to suggest what role business leaders can play in providing an environment where flow and complexity can thrive.

Unfortunately most firms are not designed to make their employees happy. Chapter 5 describes some of the most prevalent obstacles business organizations place in the way of flow. The visionary leaders interviewed for this book have all noted one or more of these pitfalls. By examining them together in this chapter, they can serve as a warning for what a hundred-year manager should seek to avoid.

In Chapter 6 the expertise of visionary leaders is called upon again to reveal how they have been able to introduce conditions in their organizations that maximize the likelihood of flow. Making work enjoyable, as we will see, contributes to greater productivity and a better morale, and most important, it supports the well-being of workers.

While the first six chapters establish the foundations for understanding happiness and how it can be either suppressed or enhanced in the workplace, the following three chapters, in Part III, delve more deeply into the question of what makes life ultimately meaningful, and what the role of leaders may be in addressing this issue. Chapter 7 argues that an enduring vision in both work and life derives its power from *soul*—the energy a person or organization devotes to purposes beyond itself. To an extent entirely unanticipated at the start of this study, all the visionary leaders drew strength and direction from goals that went well beyond what the legal requirements of their position as CEOs demanded.

Chapter 8 explores the question of how one can make all of one's life a succession of enjoyable flow experiences, unified by a coherent vision. Today's visionary leaders echo the most ancient wisdom: To be happy for life, you must first try to know yourself. Coming to learn one's strengths and weaknesses makes it possible to find the match between skills and challenges that is critical for experiencing flow. Mastering consciousness—knowing how to control one's attention and how to use one's time—are the next steps that lead to a style of leadership that improves the happiness of the leader as well as of the other members of the organization.

The argument of the book is drawn together and summarized in Chapter 9, by which point we are in the position to know what it takes to lead an organization that improves the quality of life for all concerned. As our study has shown, quite a few CEOs and managers have discovered how to implement this knowledge, and are putting it into practice daily. But there are many strong pressures that prevent more leaders from following their example. Foremost among them is the relentless expectation of increasing financial returns, which practically shackles managers at publicly held companies with the fear of being sued if they divert resources away from the single goal of raising profitability. And who would sue them? Basically, you and I. In the end, there will be no good business unless the majority comes to agree that we should demand more from business than large quarterly returns. Perhaps this book will help explain why.

Chapter 2

The Business of Happiness

Philosophers have long held that happiness is the ultimate goal of existence. Aristotle called it the *summum bonum*—the "chief good"—in that while we desire other goods, such as money or power, because we believe they will make us happy, we want happiness for its own sake. But despite centuries of debate, the questions of what happiness actually is, and whether it indeed exists, have not been resolved. Perhaps it is simply the name we give to that unattainable state where nothing else remains to be desired. Even though a state of perfect happiness may be an illusion, we all recognize that, relatively speaking, we are more satisfied, content, and joyous at some times compared to others. It is the search for such moments that constitutes each individual's *summum bonum*.

It may seem counterintuitive to argue that happiness and business have anything to do with each other, since for most people work is at best a necessary evil, and at worst, a burden. Yet the two are inextricably linked. Fundamentally, business exists to enhance human well-being. From the earliest traders carrying amber from the Baltic to the Mediterranean, salt from the coast of Africa to its interior, or spices from the islands of the Far East to the rest of the world, up to the present when new car models are heralded each year, the production and exchange of goods makes sense only if we assume that they will improve the quality of our experience.

Customers are willing to pay for products and services that they believe will make them happy. The question is, what actually *does* lead to happiness? Philosophers noticed long ago that there is no single road toward it: What brings delight to one person may well leave another person indifferent.

After almost a century of neglect, psychologists have finally summoned up the courage to address this ancient and baffling riddle. Some unexpected results have emerged. For instance, contrary to common wisdom, money and material possessions do not seem to increase happiness above a minimum threshold. In other words, if you are very poor, having more money makes you happier; if on the other hand, you are already reasonably well off, additional money does not seem to bring any significant benefit. Other studies reveal that people who experience tragedies, such as becoming blind or paralyzed, feel terrible for a few months but recover their usual level of happiness soon after. The opposite is true for those who encounter unexpected wealth: Lottery winners are happier for a few months, then revert to their former state, or even fall below it. According to some genetically oriented psychologists, such research suggests that we each have an inherited "set point" for happiness, which is more or less unaffected by external events.

Strong relationships—a stable marriage, many friends—are correlated with happiness, as is belonging to a religious community. An extroverted, optimistic temperament helps. So does having a job, and preferably a job one likes. Citizens of countries with stable, democratic governments—such as the Netherlands, Switzerland, and New Zealand—are in general also the happiest. When free elections were introduced in South Africa in 1994, the happiness of its inhabitants—and especially that of blacks—rose considerably; it has since fallen back almost to previous levels.

So what do these findings have to do with business? The answer is simple: A valuable product or service is one that customers perceive—rightly or wrongly—as making them happier. Entrepreneurial opportunities consist in discovering new ways to address this craving. Even the most sophisticated technological advances have little value until they can be demonstrated to contribute to happiness. For instance the first electronic transistors developed at Bell Labs were considered to have negligible market value, and so the patents were sold for a few thousand dollars to Sony, which had the idea of putting them into portable radios. Sony correctly reasoned that people are generally happier when they are listening to music than when they are not; hence, they would be likely to believe that if they were able to carry their music with them they would be happier than normal. In this manner an entirely new market for the advanced electronic technology, based on the desire for happiness, was created. Similar scenarios have been repeated untold times: Cars were initially envisioned as playthings, airplanes satisfied the desire to soar above the Earth before any useful function for them could be imagined, and personal computers became hugely popular at first not just because they saved time, but because of all the entertaining games one could play on them. More than we usually acknowledge, the march of technology is motivated by the hope that it will lead to happiness at the end of the rainbow.

Given the huge range of things that people believe will make them happy, however, is there some way of making sense of this diversity? As the psychologist Abraham Maslow has argued, the most basic needs are those that ensure survival—food, clothing, housing. Many people around the world are uncertain where their next meal is going to come from; for them, the satisfaction of hunger brings a measure of happiness. But for those fortunate enough not to have to worry about survival, more food or more warm clothes add only limited value. Even a 15,000-square-foot mansion with seven marble bathrooms ends up feeling like a lot of empty space.

At that point, we begin to be concerned more with security— keeping what we have, avoiding future dangers. We want a strong army; dependable police and firemen; just laws; and a stable currency. But even when such security needs are seen to, will we then be happy? Not likely. Instead, our attention will begin to shift to the need to love and be loved, to belong to a community or an entity greater than ourselves. We then begin to seek out those goods or services that promise to make us lovable—clothes, cosmetics, the soft drink advertised as the passkey to join hordes of gorgeous models having a ball at the beach. Alternatively, we join churches, clubs, or other organizations that put us in touch with some higher purpose.

Many people lead contented, relatively happy lives having achieved this level. But for others, even love and a sense of belonging begin to offer only limited satisfaction. The next gateway that beckons to the land of fulfillment is self-esteem. Some seek self-esteem in an honorable profession, a task well done, an upright family life. Others search for it in power, fame, renown—or at least in the symbols thereof: an exclusive address, expensive cars, a lifestyle that advertises "I've made it!" Feeling satisfied with oneself is quite an accomplishment, but is it the end of the road? Is this all there is? Again, for some, the answer is yes. For others, though, there is still one more option—what Maslow called self-actualization.

We are all born with a bundle of aptitudes, most of which we are not even aware of having. According to some, the highest level of happiness—self-actualization—is being able to express all the potentialities inherent in the organism. It is as if evolution has built a safety device in our nervous system that allows us to experience full happiness only when we are living at 100 percent—when we are fully using the physical and mental equipment we have been given. This mechanism would ensure that after all our other needs were taken care of, we would still seek to use the full complement of our talents, thereby making it possible not just to preserve the status quo, but also to innovate and grow.

It is not only humans who are happiest when doing what they can do best. Every organism tends toward self-actualization. Dogs bred to tend sheep are most content when herding, at which point their whole demeanor changes: they become focused and alert, hold themselves proudly, and move with grace and purpose. Hunting dogs behave similarly when stalking game (or, if all else fails, tennis balls). Dogs bred for guarding express the fullness of their being when barking at potential intruders. As the great poet Dante Alighieri wrote almost seven centuries ago: ". . . everything that is, desires to be. As we act, we unfold our being. Enjoyment naturally follows, for a thing desired always brings delight."

A business is successful to the extent that it provides a product or service that contributes to happiness in all of these forms. For instance, it may sell a car that helps to guarantee survival while using up a minimum of nonrenewable resources, that provides safety and security, that allows the owner a sense of belonging, that enhances self-esteem, and that may even provide a feeling of self-actualization by enabling the driver to express his or her unique aesthetic taste, driving skills, and particular lifestyle. The same is true of any commodity that reaches the market, from food to books, from airplane travel to banking. Its market value ultimately depends on the anticipated happiness it is expected to provide.

Another important connection between happiness and business is that one cannot engage in production and distribution alone: There is always a group of people involved, whether the concern is a small grocery store or artisan's shop or a huge conglomerate employing tens of thousands of people. A business organization whose employees are happy is more productive, has a higher morale, and has a lower turnover. Consequently, any manager who wants his or her organization to prosper should understand what makes people happy, and implement that knowledge as effectively as possible.

True and False Value

Viewed from this perspective, "good business" is not limited to the generation of profit. It refers instead to transactions that make a genuine contribution to human happiness, while "bad business" describes exchanges that do not. The difference between these two is difficult to establish precisely, because almost any product or service may make at least a few people happier than they were before. Nevertheless, it is useful to distinguish between relatively more valuable contributions, and those goods that only mimic "good" business, but provide no real, lasting satisfaction.

Although everyone who pays for a commodity does so in the expectation that the acquisition will enhance happiness, many are taken in by spurious appearances. As John Locke wrote: "In matters of happiness and misery . . . men come often to prefer the worse to the better; and to choose that which, by their own confession, has made them miserable." The reason for this, Locke thought, was that we are led into error by "how things come to be represented to our desires under deceitful appearances."

Deceit is one of the fundamental strategies for survival in the animal kingdom. It is not only among humans that a sucker is born every minute. Bears are trapped with honey, male dogs are ambushed by coyotes who send females in heat to entice them away from home, and moths fly to burn themselves in an irresistible flame. With human ingenuity we have found thousands of less drastic but no less deceitful ways to profit from the desires of our fellow men.

The most obvious forms of deception involve fraudulent claims, such as selling medicines that lack healing power, or tracts of land without water. Then there is always the temptation to resort to illegal practices such as offering bribes and payoffs and entering into collusion that restrains trade. As there are laws to protect us from such practices we need not consider them any further—everyone would agree that they are bad business. More insidious are products that do indeed produce temporary states of well-being in the user. Some of these products are legal—tobacco, alcohol, gambling—while others, such as the great variety of "recreational" drugs, are not. While such "goods" taken in moderation may improve the quality of life, when they become addictive they definitely detract from happiness in the long run.

Another kind of bad business involves the stimulation of new desires that make no significant contribution to human well-being. It is rather obvious that our current stressful lifestyle, in which many middle-class adults work increasingly long hours, is the result of craving for the symbols of a good life—newer cars, bigger houses, more expensive vacations. At the same time they forfeit the opportunity to grow as individuals, to achieve a worthwhile self-esteem, to forge close relationships.

An even more widespread form of "bad business" is enticing people to invest in schemes that while legal, are based on inflated promises that cannot be kept—such as the thousands of high-tech start-ups that went bust in the first spring of this century. Christine Comaford Lynch of Artemis Ventures has some strong words on this issue:

> High returns at any cost, I don't want to be part of that in any way, shape or form. I want to be a company builder. I don't want to take a concept public. I never want to do that. I don't want to be that opportunistic. And then exit before the widows and children get totally hosed once the stock tanks. I just don't want to do that. I see way too much of that stuff happening. It's not okay. It's, let's get richer at everybody else's expense. It's not good.

It could be argued that the economy needs such "creative destruction," which, as Schumpeter claimed, is its dynamic engine. But it should be possible to distinguish new enterprises that fail despite the fact that they were started in good faith, from those that fail because they were designed to do so.

It is naive to believe that the free market has no downside. All human institutions—whether churches or governments, whether medicine or education—need to be guarded with constant vigilance lest they become infiltrated by parasitic elements that exploit genuine needs for their own private advantage. The free market may be the best economic institution we have yet devised, but its downside is that it will supply any product for which there is sufficient demand, regardless of real benefits. In this manner a great deal of business takes advantage of the belief that more possessions will improve the quality of life, thereby contributing to the runaway materialism in our culture.

It is not that materialism in itself is bad, because up to a certain point owning and using artifacts does make us happier. Everyone is a materialist to some extent, and we wouldn't be human if we were not. But much recent research suggests that excessive concern for material possessions is unhealthy. People who score high on materialistic values tend to be more depressed, have fewer friends, less stable relationships. They are less curious, less interested in life, more easily bored. Depending on things for one's happiness leads to an ever-escalating zero-sum game: Like an addiction, it requires constant doses of acquisitions, and unless one has more "stuff" than one's neighbors, none of it ultimately counts for much.

If one were to take a radical stand, one might argue that business—the making and selling of commodities—is inherently antithetical to happiness. It is generally agreed that the best indication of whether a person is happy is that he or she no longer desires anything else. As long as we feel that we lack something, we cannot call ourselves happy. Since the purpose of business is to satisfy existing desires, or stimulate new ones, if everyone were genuinely happy, there would be no need for business any longer. In reality, however, few, if any, people have achieved the level of happiness that leaves them free of want. Because there's no reason to expect that this situation will change in the foreseeable future, business will presumably always be needed to enhance well-being.

The Two Pillars of Happiness

The total fulfillment of one's potentialities, which usually generates happiness, depends on the simultaneous presence of two processes. It is much easier to achieve happiness if one understands how these work. The first is the process of *differentiation*, which involves realizing that we are unique individuals, responsible for our own survival and well-being, who are willing to develop this uniqueness wherever it leads, while enjoying the expression of our being in action. The second process involves *integration*, or the realization that however unique we are, we are also completely enmeshed in networks of relationships with other human beings, with cultural symbols and artifacts, and with the surrounding natural environment. A person who is fully differentiated and integrated becomes a *complex* individual—one who has the best chance at leading a happy, vital, and meaningful life.

Norman Augustine, former CEO of Lockheed Martin, explained his philosophy of life in these words:

> I've always wanted to be successful. My definition of being successful is contributing something to the world . . . and being happy while doing it. . . . You have to enjoy what you are doing. You won't be very good if you don't. And secondly, you have to feel that you are contributing something worthwhile . . . if either of these ingredients [is] absent, there's probably some lack of meaning in your work.

The two components of complexity, differentiation and integration, could hardly be described more clearly than they are above. In our interviews with exemplary business leaders these same themes kept reappearing: To be successful you have to enjoy doing your best while at the same time contributing to something beyond yourself. Most of our subjects would agree with how Michael Markkula, one of the cofounders of Apple Computer, describes his attitude toward work:

> It turns out that I keep doing things that are interesting and somehow or another they make a lot of money. But that is not why I do them in the first place. That is not

why I started my company. It is not why I worked at Intel. I did it because I really enjoyed what I was doing. And there is a great deal of personal satisfaction that came from that, way more important than the money.

Clearly such entrepreneurial leaders find as much satisfaction in their jobs as any person can hope to achieve. But how many lower-level jobs allow workers to feel this way? Most work is either so dull and uninspiring that doing one's best still means using less than 10 percent of one's potentiality, or is so stressful that it sucks the worker's life energy dry. And even if they do make individual differentiation possible, many jobs fail to add to the well-being of the community.

In the chapters that follow we shall explore how to build a life and a workplace that actually enhance human growth and happiness. For the remainder of this chapter, we shall look more closely at why complexity—differentiation and integration—should be such an essential component in attaining quality in life.

The Evolution of Complexity

If we could take snapshots of what was happening on planet Earth at intervals of a few hundred thousand years, starting at its early stages as a gigantic mass of coalescing gasses, what we would see is a movement toward increasing complexity in material structures. More and more complex molecules of inanimate matter are followed by the first simple living organisms. Then the one-celled life-forms join into multicellular systems with specialized internal organs, culminating in an ever more differentiated and integrated nervous system. Finally the big brain of humans makes it possible for them to take evolution to a new level: that of culture, where more and more complex information need no longer be coded in the genes, but can be compressed in memes—units of learning contained in media such as stories, books, and computers.

Of course this enormously simplified scenario does not imply that every organism on Earth is now more complex than it was, say, a million years ago. Some species have so well adapted themselves to simple niches that they have had no incentive to become more complex; in fact, some may even find that they can survive better by becoming less differentiated or integrated than they were in the past. Because complexity requires more effort and is in many ways a more fragile state, a few species will make do with a simpler biological structure.

Nor does this scenario imply that the more complex forms now are in the majority. Clearly insects outnumber humans many times over, and the weight of their biomass is many times greater than ours. Then there is the plankton in the sea, and the enormous variety of bacteria and viruses that go about their business happily while using humans as their feeding and breeding ground.

Finally the evolution of complexity up to this point offers no guarantees that it will continue forever, or even until next year. The more complex a system gets to be, the more improbable it becomes, the more things can go wrong with it, and the more effort it takes to keep it from decaying. For example, the cascading effects of the terrorist acts of September 11, 2001, provide a clear warning about how vulnerable a complex society can become. The specialization and concentration of the organs of government, transportation, and communication and of the supplies of water and food can present an increasingly tempting target to even a few well-trained individuals. And if the complex human brain convinces itself that it needs increasing amounts of material resources to be happy, it could lead easily to such a devastation of the environment that only simpler organisms—like the supremely adapted cockroach—will be able to thrive in it.

Nevertheless, it is safe to say that at no point in our series of snapshots taken thousands of years apart would we find an earlier time in which there existed an organism that was more differentiated and integrated than those in the following frame. In other words, evolution has been proceeding toward the peak of complexity—and whether we like it or not, that peak at present is us. Whether evolution will continue to produce more complex forms in the future is now our responsibility. We can either help to make this world a more incredible place than it has ever been, or we can hasten its return to inorganic dust.

Complexity and the Life Cycle

It is not only on the mind-boggling scale of planetary evolution that complexity plays such an important role. Much closer to our own experience, it is also the essence of what takes place over time in each person's life. One can view human development as a series of pendulum swings between agency and communion; between seeking uniqueness and needing to belong to something greater and more powerful. The first stage of this process of growth begins when babies first realize how weak and vulnerable they are. At that point—sometime in the first year of life—it becomes very important for them to get attached to their mother or another powerful parental figure.

But after a year or so of intense dependence, infants begin to feel the need to assert their autonomy. At some level they sense that unless they begin to take charge of their actions they will never grow up into fully functioning persons. Consequently, they insist on doing things their own way, and if they are prevented from doing so, they are ready to throw tantrums—it is the classic age of the "terrible twos." A few individuals stop their development at this point, but their self-centeredness and impulsivity usually mark them in the eyes of the majority as immature sociopaths.

As they grow to realize the vastness of the world outside their homes most children eventually become again intimidated by their own insignificance. At that point, they become concerned with fitting in with their peers, with being accepted and recognized by a community larger than the family. This is the stage of conformity, and for a great many people it is the end of the road in personal development.

By the time the biological changes of puberty begin, however, many teenagers are no longer content with being merely conformists. Individuality again becomes an important goal, and when it is too difficult to achieve, rebellion will take its place. Some may eventually return to a safe conformity, others will alternate between being rebels and conformists, and a few will keep searching for their identity indefinitely.

A dwindling number of people in each successive age group may follow further swings of the pendulum that go from the assertion of individuality to the acceptance of group values. Some psychologists have detected as many as ten stages, each involving either an external or an internal priority, each more complex than the one before it because it involves a more pronounced individuation and a deeper integration. The end point—the highest level of development—is one at which a person has refined her uniqueness and is in control of her thoughts, feelings, and actions, while at the same time relishing human diversity, and feeling at one with the infinite cosmos. A person who has reached this stage can truly be called happy, because she needs nothing more.

Business and Human Development

In a typical organization, one will find people whose development has reached any of the stages described above. A few—and sometimes this includes the leaders of the firm—will not have progressed beyond the impulsive stage of the terrible twos. Such individuals are often successful in environments where ruthlessness and risk taking are valued. They may even attract admiration with their self-assurance masquerading as charisma.

The majority of employees is likely to be content to follow the rules without rocking the boat. Such conformity is generally welcome in many organizations. But in a rapidly changing, competitive environment more is needed. Knowledge workers, especially, tend to value their autonomy, and need scope for initiative and growth. Some of them will be loners, some rebels, and a few will have achieved that fine blend of individuality and cooperation that is the endpoint and fulfillment of personal development.

Whatever the composition of a firm, if it is to do good business it should be a place where everyone is encouraged to progress toward complexity—or at the very least a place that does not make it more difficult to achieve personal growth. Contrary to common perception, there are many successful executives who understand that "good business" involves more than making money, and who take the responsibility for making their firms an engine for enhancing the quality of life. Often these individuals base their actions on religious principles, or they develop their values along the lines of what might be called secular humanism.

For example, Richard DeVos, the CEO of Amway, draws inspiration for running his business from a feeling of responsibility to a Christian God, which permeates all his relationships and trickles down to his workers:

> I'm responsible to God. Then I'm responsible to my wife. I am responsible to my family and to my community, and to the people who are involved in my companies, who look to us for encouragement, support, sound decisions, respect. Respect is a big factor ... There's only certain things that are right and other things that are wrong. Then once you establish that, it's not really difficult.

Aaron Feuerstein, the owner and CEO of Malden Mills, became something of a celebrity a few years ago, when his factory in Massachusetts burned down. Despite the loss he continued to pay the wages of his unemployed workers until the factory was back in operation many months later. Feuerstein draws the values that inform his actions from a Jewish heritage:

> I'm trying to make a blend of two strategies that are not blended here in the United States. One is maximizing

the profit of the shareholders, and the other is trying to do something worthwhile on this Earth, not only for the shareholders but for the employees, community, environment . . . You work real hard in business and there's a ruthless kind of principle in business . . . It's a battle for money and it's a battle for profits, and it has nothing to do with trying to do good, or what's right on this Earth. That's relegated to when you go home . . . and if you are so inclined, you could be charitable to others. . . . But I don't think of it that way. I think of it more in my religious Jewish upbringing, that doing good and being of service to other people, mitzvah, is the greatest good deed one can do.

While traditional religious values are often the basis for realizing that good business is a much more involved proposition than just making a profit, some individuals arrive at the same conclusion as the result of a more tortuous personal quest. For instance Jane Fonda, who has been successful at several business enterprises, formulates her understanding of the importance of growth on the basis of physics:

People are capable, including myself, of perpetual change and growth. It's the one thing in the entire universe that goes counter to the second law of thermodynamics—entropy—everything descends into decay. Everything spirals downward, rots and decays, except the human spirit, which has the capacity to grow and to evolve upward.

The wisdom of traditional religions, and an understanding of evolution as the process whereby entropy is temporarily reversed, both yield the same conclusion for our purposes: Business that does not contribute to human growth and well-being is not worth doing, no matter how much profit it generates in the short run.

The only debate involved is about how broadly one should define the term "well-being." Those committed to a strict free-market position insist that a CEO is responsible only for the financial well-being of those who own shares in the business he runs. Any other consideration is a distraction from the CEO's duties, and cause for dismissal. This narrow interpretation is challenged by all the executives we interviewed. Somewhere at the other end of the spectrum is the position voiced by Leon Gorman, the chairman of the outdoor equipment and clothing maker L.L.Bean:

> [Our goal is to] completely fulfill our responsibilities to all our stakeholders . . . our customers, employees, management group, owners; our communities and our natural environment. And also our vendors . . . We do not believe in profit maximization or maximization of shareholder value. We believe in optimizing the value that we create, and we add to the lives of all our stakeholders. [Our goal is] adding to the quality of life of our customers through our product, service, and similarly, adding to the quality of life for our employees: in individual development, job security, and dealing with their aspirations.

Gorman's position, and that of the other leaders who participated in our studies—who are in turn only a small sample of the many responsible businessmen working in the world—is not just a pious platitude concocted for public relation purposes. These are people who walk the walk, often risking their jobs at the hand of greedy investors. Does that make them idealistic martyrs who suffer for the well-being of others? This does not seem to be the case. Making complexity happen is a joyous business. Individuals who are driven by the desire to do their best, and to contribute most widely to society, believe in what they are doing, and are happy doing it. What more can one ask?

Chapter 3

Happiness in Action

C ontrary to what most of us believe, happiness does not simply happen to us. It's something that *we* make happen, and it results from our doing our best. Feeling fulfilled when we live up to our potentialities is what motivates differentiation and leads to evolution. The experience of happiness in action is *enjoyment*—the exhilarating sensation of being fully alive. Seeking out pleasure is also a powerful source of motivation, but pleasure does not foster change; it is, rather, a conservative force, one that makes us want to satisfy existing needs, to achieve an equilibrium, comfort, and relaxation. There is nothing inherently wrong with seeking pleasure, but the person for whom it becomes the main reason for living is not going to grow beyond what genes have programmed him to desire.

Enjoyment, on the other hand, is not always pleasant, and it can be very stressful at times. A mountain climber, for example, may be close to freezing, utterly exhausted, and in danger of falling into a bottomless crevasse, yet he wouldn't want to be anywhere else. Sipping a piña colada under a palm tree at the edge of the turquoise ocean is idyllic, but it just doesn't compare to the exhilaration he feels on that windswept ridge. Chess players continue to play, despite the fact that at the end of a day's tournament they can barely stand up from the table, and are coping with an aching head and a bursting bladder. Dancers sacrifice their entire lives to the iron discipline of their art, giving up relationships, parenthood, and most of the other pleasures of life in order to excel in it. At the moment it is experienced, enjoyment can be both physically painful and mentally taxing; but because it involves a triumph over the forces of entropy and decay, it nourishes the spirit. Enjoyment is the foundation for memories that, in retrospect, enrich lives, and give confidence for facing the future. In terms of the individual lifespan, then, the consequences of enjoyment are quite different from those derived from pleasure.

It is impossible to survive as a leader in business without enjoying what one does. The job would become too stressful, the hours too long, and the temptation to spend more and more time on diversions too strong. In our interviews people were quite specific in describing their attitudes toward their work. For instance, the CEO of one of the world's largest multinational companies said:

> It's an enormous responsibility and it's an enormous challenge. And it's the most fun job in the world! I love coming to work every morning. I can't wait to get here. I can't wait, because every day something else is going to happen.

Like many others, Deborah Besemer, CEO of BrassRing Systems, was attracted to a business career by the enjoyment of it: "I'd started to have other friends, too, that had graduated a couple years before me, and they were having fun in the business world, and I had never thought of the business world as being much fun. And fun's important." One finds almost universally among successful business leaders the same enthusiasm for their work. This leads us to examine in greater depth the question: What does it actually *mean* to enjoy something?

The Experience of Flow

Studies conducted around the world these last few decades have shown that in whatever context people feel a deep sense of enjoyment, they describe that experience in very similar terms. Regardless of age, gender, or education, they report the same mental state. What they are actually doing at the time is wildly different—they may be meditating, running a race, playing chess, or performing surgery—but what they feel at the moment is remarkably consistent. I have given the name "flow" to this common experience, because so many people have used the analogy of being carried away by an outside force, of moving effortlessly with a current of energy, at the moments of highest enjoyment.

What follows are some excerpts from interviews we collected over the years that provide some glimpses of the subjective state of flow. The first is from an expert rock climber who describes his mental state when climbing:

> The task at hand is so demanding and rich in its complexity and pull . . . one tends to get immersed in what is going on around him, in the rock, in the moves that are involved . . . [in the] search for handholds . . . [and the] proper position of the body—[he becomes] so involved he might lose consciousness of his own identity and melt into the rock.

Now compare his account with that of a surgeon describing why his job is so enjoyable:

> In good surgery everything you do is essential, every move is excellent and necessary; there is elegance, little blood loss, and a minimum of trauma . . . This is very pleasant, particularly when the group works together in a smooth and efficient manner.

Both individuals describe one of the basic elements of flow: The task at hand draws one in with its complexity to such an extent that one becomes completely involved in it. There is no distinction between thought and action, between self and environment. The important thing is to execute each move as well as possible, because lives may depend on it.

These dramatic examples notwithstanding, flow does not require a life-and-death setting to be enjoyable. The most widely reported flow activity the world over is reading a good book, during which one becomes immersed in the characters and their vicissitudes to the point of forgetting oneself. Remarkably often, flow is also experienced while at work, as recounted by this seventy-six-year-old woman who still farms in the Italian Alps:

> It gives me a great satisfaction, to be outdoors, to talk with people, to be with my animals . . . I talk to everybody—plants, birds, flowers, and animals. Everything in nature keeps you company, you see nature progress each day. You feel clean and happy: too bad you get tired and have to go home . . . Even when you have to work a lot it is very beautiful.

This woman describes her work almost in terms of a romantic idyll, despite the fact that she gave her account after walking several miles down a mountain meadow carrying on her back a bale of hay twice as tall as she is. Nevertheless, by paying attention to the complexity of the natural world around her, she was able to become at one with it, and to enjoy it. Often a flow experience is the result of spending time with others in a close interaction. Here is a mother describing her most precious moments:

> when I'm working with my daughter, when she is discovering something new. A new cookie recipe that she has accomplished, that she has made herself, an artistic work that she has done that she's proud of. Her reading

is one thing that she's really into, and we read together. She reads to me, and I read to her, and that's a time when I sort of lose touch with the rest of the world, I'm totally absorbed in what I am doing.

Paying attention to one's daughter, watching her grow and discover new things, and responding to the many changes in her personality appropriately require as much skill as it takes to be a good rock climber, farmer, or surgeon. Immersion in such a complex activity enables one's own self in turn to become stronger and more complex.

But are such experiences relevant to business? According to the successful executives we interviewed, flow can definitely take place in the work environment. Some believe flow is even a necessity, because if one doesn't enjoy one's job, one can't be very good at it. As Orit Gadiesh, CEO of Bain & Co., says: "Having fun with what you do is important. You can't just sort of say: 'Well, I'm going to work all these hours and then I'm going to have fun.' " Like the work of the surgeon, or that of the mountain farmer, most businesses do provide enough opportunities to compel one's attention. Mike Murray, who at the time of his interview was vice president for human resources at Microsoft, observes:

> Living is so fun, and I see work as one element of that. I want to be able to love work because I have to spend so much time in it. I better enjoy it! . . . I also really like the business of business. . . . Business is fun for me.

Norman Augustine of Lockheed Martin has a similar opinion:

> [You'll be happy] . . . if you are doing well what you are doing today and if you're enjoying it . . . let the future take care of itself . . . you have to know that you have a direction that you want to go in, but then I think you have to sort of drift with the opportunity.

But what is the precise nature of this enjoyment that these people are describing? In a series of other studies, I and my colleagues around the world interviewed close to ten thousand individuals in all walks of life and discovered that a person's consciousness when he or she is genuinely enjoying the moment—that is, having a flow experience—can be described in terms of eight conditions. Not all of them inevitably accompany flow, and their relative importance may vary, but by and large they are the most salient components of what it feels like to be in flow. Let us review them one by one.

How Does It Feel to Be in Flow?

1. Goals Are Clear. For a person to become deeply involved in any activity it is essential that he know precisely what tasks he must accomplish, moment by moment. For instance, what involves the rock climber is not the ultimate goal of reaching the top of the mountain, but the immediate task of making the next move without falling. The goal that keeps the chess player concentrated is not winning the game, but achieving the most strategic position with the next move or series of moves. A mother gets "totally absorbed" in reading with her daughter not because she is concerned that her daughter be well educated, but because when they are together she wants to respond to every turn of her daughter's body and mind. Of course the ultimate goals of these activities—reaching the summit, winning the game, getting a child to love reading—are also important but true enjoyment comes from the steps one takes toward attaining a goal, not from actually reaching it.

People often miss the opportunity to enjoy what they do because they focus all their attention on the outcome, rather than savoring the steps along the way. Where does the pleasure in singing come from—finishing the song, or producing each note or phrase? Do we appreciate a fine dinner because we feel full at its end, or because each bite has tasted good? Isn't negotiating a business deal more satisfying than signing it?

To be overly concerned with the ultimate goal often interferes with performance. If a tennis player thinks only of winning the match, she won't be able to respond to her opponent's powerful serve. The salesman who is too concerned with earning his commission, and is not sufficiently attentive to the buyer's moods, is less likely to make the sale. Again, our primary concern here is not with what constitutes a successful performance, but with the quality of experience *during* performance. If we agree that the bottom line of life is happiness, not success, then it makes perfect sense to say that it is the journey that counts, not reaching the destination.

2. Feedback Is Immediate. It is difficult for people to stay absorbed in any activity unless they get timely, "online" information about how well they are doing. The sense of total involvement of the flow experience derives in large part from knowing that what one does matters, that it has consequences. Feedback may come from colleagues or supervisors who comment on performance, but preferably it is the activity itself that will provide this information.

For example, a climber doesn't have to worry whether or not his moves are successful as long as he is still hanging safely onto the rock. Surgeons depend on more subtle but to them equally obvious signals: "You get a feeling when things aren't going well. There will be supply problems, and the tissues will not be rejoined properly." Or: "You rely entirely on precise, immediate feedback . . ." "I sense the correctness by the way things look." A mother can tell from behavioral signs when her daughter becomes bored or distracted, and can change her approach until the child is involved again.

Some individuals have developed such strong internal standards that they no longer need the opinion of others to judge whether they have performed a task well or not. The ability to give objective feedback to oneself is in fact the mark of the expert.

Among the most difficult activities to enjoy are those that involve creative work, like painting a picture or writing a story, because there are no standard criteria with which to evaluate performance. A writer may think that what he has just composed is great, but is it really? Unless he learns to trust his internal standards, based on knowledge and past experience, his efforts will lead to misery rather than satisfaction. On the other hand, the joy of knowing for certain that one has accomplished something never done before is beyond compare.

3. A Balance Between Opportunity and Capacity. It is easier to become completely involved in a task if we believe it is doable. If it appears to be beyond our capacity we tend to respond to it by feeling anxious; if the task is too easy we get bored. In either case attention shifts from what needs to be accomplished—the anxious person is distracted by worries about the outcome, while the bored one starts searching for other things to do. The ideal condition can be expressed by the simple formula: *Flow occurs when both challenges and skills are high and equal to each other.*

However, be aware that "ideal" is a judgment that depends on the context: What is challenging to one person may not be so for anyone else. Few people regard a sheer wall of rock as an opportunity; most will simply ignore it. Surgeons are not likely to find psychiatry challenging (an analyst may have to treat a patient for years, with little apparent improvement), and vice versa (surgery does not require any thinking, merely manual dexterity—the same skills needed to fix a car engine). Similarly, and unfortunately, many parents fail to respond to the opportunity of understanding their children—or they are daunted by it. Whether or not a person responds to an opportunity depends in part on the skills he has either inherited or learned. A naturally well-coordinated, athletic child will be drawn to sports, while a child whose parents take news seriously and discuss current events around the dinner table may grow up to find journalism or politics challenging.

A good flow activity is one that offers challenges at several levels of complexity. A rock climber elaborates on this point: "There are days when you're not up to perfection, when you want to mellow out on some easy rock; others when you're quite willing to maim yourself for all time." Likewise activities that are good at producing flow are not easy to exhaust, for they have a high ceiling of complexity: "Obviously you're not going to reach any perfection in climbing because your mind is always one step ahead . . . You can always think of one step more perfect that you can do . . . It's an endless moving up."

The complexity of the challenges they face is one of the reasons surgeons love their work: "It's very satisfying, and if it is somewhat difficult it is also exciting . . . An unusual case is most satisfying—*particularly when the patient does well.*" The italicized sentiment is worth noting: What is most gratifying to this particular surgeon—and to most others we interviewed—is to perform a difficult operation well. The patient's recovery is almost of secondary importance. This may sound callous to an outsider, but it makes very good sense: A surgeon cannot control the reactions of the patient's body, but only the specifics of the operation itself. From that perspective, it's in everyone's best interest that his first priority should be doing the best job possible, with the hope that the patient's organism will also cooperate.

As skills improve, one is able to take on greater challenges. In fact, one must do so, to prevent tasks from becoming routine and boring. The very experience of flow thus becomes one incentive for growing to higher levels of complexity. How this works is well described by the Pardeys, two sailors who like to travel around the globe either alone or as a couple:

> The pride you'll feel as your skills develop can't be easily described. The first time you sail your six-tonner up to the dock so she stops within a foot of the cleats, the first hatch you build that doesn't leak a drop, the first repair job you successfully complete—each is a triumph that

will bring a glow to your life. Eventually this self-sufficiency will grow to be a sport. You'll set new goals and reach them.

In everyday existence, most people find it difficult to achieve such "triumphs." They find their jobs too confining, their family life too predictable or too daunting. In response they search for the balance of challenges and skills in activities like sports, hobbies, or travel—or perhaps in outlets like illicit relationships or "recreational" drugs. Yet the fact is that *any* activity can produce flow, because hidden in even the most seemingly mundane tasks—working on the assembly line, talking to one's child, or washing dishes—are opportunities for using one's skills.

Even in the most horrible circumstances some people are able to find opportunities to exercise their skills and enter flow. Abandoned to their own resources, prisoners in solitary confinement have learned to develop mental games with which to keep themselves focused. Solzhenitsyn describes one who held on to his sanity by taking an imaginary trip from Moscow to America. He measured the length of his cell, and every day walked a few kilometers from wall to wall, visualizing the landscape along the way. By the time he was removed to another prison, he had made it halfway across the Atlantic. When physical escape is not possible, one has the resources to imagine a better virtual world of one's making.

Of all human talents, among the most precious ones is this ability to discern opportunities around oneself, when others do not. In a given situation, one person will say "there is nothing to do," whereas another will find dozens of things to do and enjoy. The individual who is truly engaged with the world—interested, curious, excited—is never at a loss for opportunities to experience flow.

4. Concentration Deepens. When we begin to respond to an opportunity that has clear goals and provides immediate feedback, we are likely to become involved in it, even if the activity itself is not very "important"—such as a game, a hobby, or a stimulating conversation. When the involvement passes a certain threshold of intensity, we suddenly find ourselves deeply *into* the game, the pursuit, or the interaction. We no longer have to think about what to do, but act spontaneously, almost automatically, even when some aspect of the task at hand is very difficult or dangerous.

In everyday life, as we move through the day from morning to night, we rarely concentrate our attention beyond a very brief and superficial level. Instead we are constantly distracted, our attention flitting from one stimulus to the next, like the "monkey mind" the Buddhists describe. Such chronic distraction makes it difficult to experience the wholeness of our being. In flow, however, action and awareness merge in a seamless wave of energy. A rock climber describes the process as follows:

> It's a Zen feeling, like meditation or concentration. One thing you're after is the one-pointedness of mind. . . . when things become automatic . . . somehow the right thing is done without your ever thinking about it or doing anything at all . . . it just happens. And you are more concentrated . . .

In those moments the distinction between self and activity disappears. In the words of an elite racer: "It doesn't seem like you're sitting on a bike. You feel like it's just one piece of machinery working together . . . like you are part of this machine that you were born with . . ." Another climber explains: "It's a pleasant feeling of total involvement. You become like a robot . . . no, more like an animal . . . getting lost in kinesthetic sensation . . . a panther powering up the rock." This is a peculiar kind of concentration, because one does not have to force the mind to think hard, as when trying to solve a math problem; on the contrary, the process seems effortless. The poet Richard Jones puts it well:

> I just feel like there's energy going through and I'm just
> not blocking it, not getting in the way of it. A very intel-
> ligent energy flows through the body when you write,
> and it's the energy that is concentrated and translated,
> not the mind. Flow occurs when I don't let the writer in
> me get in the way of writing. How do I get in the way? I
> start thinking.

At the point "thinking" begins, the fusion of writer and writing is broken. The poet tries to shape ideas into words self-consciously, instead of letting them bubble up and arrange themselves in an order of their own making. By contrast, in flow the poet concentrates on the words that emerge from his mind—savoring, cherishing, struggling to fathom their meaning—rather than forcing them to do his bidding. An ace basketball player describes his most intense moments similarly: "I have found myself at times when I have super concentration in a game whereby nothing else exists—nothing exists except the act of participating and swinging the ball. [The other player must] be there to play the game, but I'm not concerned with him. I'm not competing with him at that point. I'm attempting to place the ball in the perfect spot, and it has no bearing on winning or losing."

Concentration in flow can be so deep that the term "ecstasy" is sometimes used to describe it. In Greek *ecstasy* meant literally "to stand to the side"; in its figurative sense it likewise means to be standing outside everyday routine life in a separate reality defined by the rules and demands of an activity. Some find ecstasy by actually moving from one space to another—into a temple, a museum, a majestic natural setting. As one climber puts it: "There is great potential when man is on the mountain. People are always searching through booze, drugs, whatever. The closest man can come to it is through nature. Mountaineering builds up body and mind while learning about the deepest chasms of man. Up there you see man's true place in nature, you feel one with nature." Others attain ecstasy while sitting at their desk, letting their mind move into a different world where only numbers, verses, chess problems, or musical notes exist. Ralph Shapey, a well-known contemporary composer, said:

> You are in an ecstatic state to such a point that you feel as though you don't exist. I've experienced this time and time again. My hand seems devoid of myself, and I have nothing to do with what is happening. I just sit there watching it in a state of awe and wonderment. And [the music] just flows out by itself.

It is interesting to note that ecstasy is really the result of our limited ability to concentrate. Our mind cannot cope with too many stimuli simultaneously. If we really focus attention on a given task—whether climbing or writing music—we cannot notice anything outside that narrow stimulus field.

5. The Present Is What Matters. Because in flow the task at hand demands complete attention, the worries and problems that are so nagging in everyday life have no chance to register in the mind. It is for this reason that an enjoyable experience produces an ecstatic state, the sensation of being in a different world. For the chess player, this world becomes limited to the pieces on the board and their respective fields of force; for a composer, the world is made up of little black marks on paper and the sounds they represent. The world of flow is limited not only in space, but also in time: because attention must be focused on the present, events from the past or the future cannot find room in consciousness. A mountaineer who is a physicist in "real" life gives a very specific account: "When I start a climb, it is as if my memory input has been cut off. All I can remember is the last thirty seconds, and all I can think ahead is the next five minutes." An African American teenager from the inner city who plays basketball concurs: "When the game is exciting, I don't seem to hear anything—the world seems to be cut off from me and all there is to think about is my game."

The human mind is programmed to turn to threats, to unfinished business, to failures and unfulfilled desires when it has nothing else more urgent to do, when attention is left free to wander. Without a task to focus our attention, most of us find ourselves getting progressively depressed. In flow there is no room for such rumination: "The hang-ups that I have are momentarily obliterated. . . . It's one of the few ways I have found to live outside my head," says a climber about what makes his sport so attractive.

This feature of flow may at first seem to resemble suspiciously what we would ordinarily call an "escape mechanism." It is true that flow does provide a relief from obsessively dwelling on unpleasant thoughts, much as more familiar forms of escape— alcohol, drugs, promiscuous sex—provide. But the consequences are quite different. Because flow involves meeting challenges and developing skills, it leads to growth. It is an escape *forward* from current reality, whereas stimulants like drugs lead backward. Albert Einstein once said that art and science were the best means to escape from reality that humanity had devised, and his insight applies to other sources of flow equally well.

6. Control Is No Problem. When people describe their flow experiences, one of the first things they mention is a strong sense of being in control of the situation. In everyday life, we are constantly exposed to events over which we have no say: A careless driver on the freeway, an erratic boss, a slumping economy. In the clearly circumscribed world of a flow activity, we know that as long as we respect its challenges and develop the appropriate skills to meet them, we stand a good chance of being able to cope with the situation. Some people, like the chess player quoted above, even experience it as an ability to control others: "I get a tyrannical sense of power. I feel immensely strong, as though I have the fate of another human in my grasp. I want to kill!"

In general, though, the feeling is more benign, and has more to do with the ability to control one's own performance than the environment itself. As a basketball player describes it: "I feel in control, sure. I've practiced and have a good feeling for the shots I can make. . . . I don't feel in control of the other player—even if he is bad and I know where to beat him. It's me and not him that I'm working on." An Olympic runner's account is typical:

> It is being totally in control of your own body and how hard you are pushing, and to be able to go faster when you say, "Okay, let's put on a bit of a sprint and drop this person." And being in total control of what's going through your head. Like if pain comes to you, to be able to say "Okay, fine, I expected this. That's all right, I'm not going to dwell on it. . . . total mental and physical control."

"Total control" of one's own mind is in fact too strong an expression to describe accurately what happens when one is in flow. The point is not that one can always do what one wants, but rather that the possibility of making things happen as one wishes is present in a way that seldom occurs in "real" life. The poet Marvin Bell puts it well:

> [Am I] more or less in control when in flow? I don't think about it. I am out of this world. Am I more in control of the other world? I wouldn't call it control because it's a confidence that comes from surrendering to the materials rather than controlling them. Of course I "control" by making choices, but the rationale for the choices is poetic rather than sensible.

What Bell is saying is that it is the aesthetic requirements of the verse itself that dictate what words he should use. The poet thus becomes a conduit for the expression of poetry; the words flow through him. Many others describe their experience as that of becoming a vessel, of being inspired, of becoming possessed by the Muse. But this is true not only of art. All flow activities have their own specific logic and beauty, so that when acting according to their rules, it is difficult to ascertain who is in control—the actor, or the script. Surrender to the requirements of the situation is a feature of flow even in physical activities where control would seem to be a matter of necessity. In the words of a rock climber: "You aren't really the master, but are moving with something else. That's the part where the really good feeling comes from. You are moving in harmony with something else, the piece of rock as well as the weather and the scenery. You're part of it and thus lose some of the feeling of individual separation."

In the ordinary mind-set of everyday life we typically feel that we need to be in control out of a fear that others will take advantage of us. From that perspective the mantra of Andy Grove, chairman of Intel—"Only the paranoids survive"—makes sense. It is in such a world that one values the leadership secrets of Attila the Hun, reads *The Art of War*, and seeks to adopt Machiavelli's stratagems; power, control, and mastery seem nothing less than necessary survival tactics. But the very same situation will appear quite different if a person is viewing it from a state of flow. Then one needs no longer be in control of a deal, a budget, or a board meeting, for what matters is doing one's best for the sake of the task at hand, and having confidence that the best will be enough to prevail.

7. The Sense of Time Is Altered. One typical element of the flow experience is that time is experienced differently. Quite often, this means that time is perceived as flying by. A chess player comments: "Time passes a hundred times faster. In this sense, it resembles the dream state. A whole story can unfold in seconds, it seems." A surgeon agrees: "Time is totally distorted—faster—[what] seems like fifteen minutes [has] been two hours."

A good example of this phenomenon comes from my personal experience. The last time I saw my half brother Moricz before he passed away was in his small apartment in Budapest. Moricz was twenty years older than I, and his life had not been easy. Before

WWII he felt obliged to work at a profession he didn't particularly like in order to support his growing family, and after the war he was taken for six years to the Soviet gulags, which he barely survived. After he was released, despite his degrees from the universities of Geneva and Rome, the only job he could find for many years was as a stoker on the railroads. He never complained, never faltered in his commitment to the family or to his ideals. It was not until he was in his eighties that he was finally able to indulge in the intellectual passion of his life: the collection of crystals. He read trade magazines, traveled to see dealers, and attended conventions; he transformed his living room into a museum with shelves running from floor to ceiling along all four walls, and installed spotlights to illuminate rare specimens from all the world's continents.

As we inspected his collection, Moricz lifted a small rock, about the size of a small apple, from its stand. "I was looking at this thing just yesterday," he said, smiling. "It was nine in the morning when I put it under the microscope. Outside it was sunny, just like today. I kept turning the rock around, looking at all the fissures, the intrusions, the dozen or more different crystal formations inside and around . . . then I looked up, and thought that a storm must be coming, because it had gotten so dark . . . then I realized that it was not overcast, but the sun had been setting—it was past seven in the evening."

The piece of rock he was holding was indeed beautiful, almost a mountain in miniature, riddled with caves ablaze with tiny rainbow-hued stalagmites. I could imagine myself becoming preoccupied with looking at it for five minutes or so. But several *hours?* That was inconceivable. The difference between us was that Moricz had developed the knowledge to decode every speck, every grain of the rock. While to my untutored eyes it was merely an interesting piece of stone, for him it was as fascinating and as richly detailed as a book. He could determine its chemical composition, the physical forces involved in shaping the rock, the kind of environment it came from, the geography of the region, the history of its discovery and the possible uses of its ingredients. When he brought his decoding skills in contact with the information that was latent in the rock, it sparked an episode of flow during which time stood dramatically still.

In some cases the opposite effect takes place, and time seems to expand rather than contract. Many athletes would recognize their own experiences in that of Donovan Bailey, world record holder for the fifty-meter race and former Olympic champion in the one-hundred-meter event, who says that the 9.8 seconds it takes him to run the race feel like an eternity. Similarly the writer Peter Davison reports: "Five minutes of pure attention to an emerging poem is longer than a week of clocks and hours." The climber Doug Robinson remarks of a difficult move on a climb: "It is said to be only a moment, yet by virtue of total absorption . . . the winds of eternity blow through it."

Robinson's analysis is correct: The speed at which time passes depends on "absorption," that is, on how focused the mind is. The reason we assume that all time intervals are the same is that we have invented clocks that measure time as if that were the case— sixty seconds to a minute, sixty minutes to an hour. But in reality we experience time far more subjectively, so that at various times it seems to speed up, slow down, or stand still. In flow, the sense of time adapts itself to the action at hand.

There are activities where knowing the time precisely, instead of interfering with flow, is a condition for experiencing it. For instance, some highly specialized surgeons, who have to move smoothly from one operation to the next so that they can begin work on a patient at exactly the right moment, after all the preparatory work has been done by the operating team, comment: "I always know what time it is . . . I sense the time to the minute," or, "I know what time it is subconsciously. I sense what time it is very closely to the minute." For them, the ability to tell clock time intuitively is one of the skills that must be acquired in order to experience flow.

A good summary of flow's altered sense of time is provided by an Olympic figure skater: "Time does quicken and slow; it seems like it almost bends at your will . . . For instance, if you're more in focus, it will slow down. And if you're feeling really good about something really difficult, something that usually takes a long time, it goes by very quickly." In other words, rather than having to chase the clock and constantly worry what time it is, we come to learn that we ourselves control the subjective experience of the passage of time.

8. The Loss of Ego. Many of the descriptions of flow quoted up to now have mentioned the fact that while immersed in the experience one tends to forget not only one's problems and surroundings, but one's very self. It is as if awareness of one's personhood were temporarily suspended. This is another result of the intense focusing of attention that pushes anything not directly related to the task at hand out of consciousness.

The climber Dennis Eberl, recounting a difficult ascent of the Matterhorn, speaks of those "rare moments of almost orgiastic unity as I forget myself and become lost in action." Clearly the climber does not "forget" himself in the sense of becoming unaware of his position, or the placement of his fingers and toes on the vertical surface; in fact he is probably much *more* aware of his body and its functions than he is when off the rock. Neither does the surgeon or the pianist become unaware of his fingers, or the chess player of the strategies jostling in her mind. What they do forget is their social personae—name, rank, and serial number, so to speak—with all the responsibilities these entail. It is an exhilarating feeling to be momentarily relieved of self-consciousness, of one's ambitions and defeats, fears and desires.

If that feeling is not always so deep as to warrant the description of "orgiastic unity," it is frequently one of belonging to some greater entity, whether a tradition or the "harmony of the spheres" that is often mentioned by musical performers as the peculiar order in consciousness they experience while playing. Or it can merely be the satisfying sense that one belongs to an efficient group working toward the same purpose: "Surgery is a team effort.

But it's like basketball: You don't have to stop and look around to see where the ball is; you know how things are by the way the motion is going. You fade out of the awareness of the team only in the most difficult times."

Western cultures differ from those of the rest of the world in emphasizing individuality, autonomy, and the separation of the self from its social matrix. Yet as human beings we continue to need the feeling that we belong to a community, to an entity greater than ourselves. Our daily lives offer few opportunities to experience this feeling, and then often only in settings where we are more or less passive audience members at a public performance, such as a concert, a sports event, a religious service, or political rally. Thus the transcendence of individuality that flow makes possible provides a rare chance to take an active involvement in something larger than the self, without relinquishing any of one's mental, physical, or volitional skills.

While one typically forgets the self during the flow experience, after the event a person's self-esteem reappears in a stronger form than it had been before. When measurements are taken of variations in self-esteem during the day, one finds that after approaching a flowlike state a person's self-esteem score climbs significantly. Similarly, people who have more flow experiences also have higher self-esteem overall. While unexpected, this paradoxical finding is not really that surprising. Half a century ago, the Austrian psychiatrist Viktor Frankl wrote that happiness cannot be attained by wanting to be happy—it must come as the unintended consequence of working for a goal greater than oneself. The truth of this insight is borne out by our own findings.

Why Do It?

The results of taking part in a flow activity may be as consequential as saving lives, as in the case of the surgeon, or as personal as coming up with a beautiful poem or piece of music. While both are worthy goals, they are not even necessary, for when a task produces flow, it is worth doing for its own sake. A famous composer remarked: "This is what I tell my students: 'Don't expect to make money, don't expect fame or a pat on the back, don't expect a damn thing. Do it because you love it.' " The Buddhist saying expresses this same sentiment, "You are entitled to the work, but not to its rewards." This is, admittedly, not a very popular way of thinking in our world, where everyone is concerned about his rights and entitlements. Of course, we naturally all want to receive what we consider our just rewards, and should do our best to get them. But if we do not enjoy the work that leads to them, we are forfeiting the most important part of the deal.

Something that is worth doing for its own sake is called autotelic (from the Greek *auto* = self and *telos* = goal), because it contains its goal within itself. We don't need external rewards to pursue such activities; we don't require payment or admiration to play the guitar, hike in the woods, or read a good novel. Another way to term such activities is *intrinsically rewarding*, because their primary reward is simply in being involved with them. Contrast these with activities that are primarily *exotelic* or *extrinsically rewarding*, which we do only with the expectation of some gain, or to avoid being punished. Schoolwork for young people and paid work for adults are often extrinsically motivated.

There are very few activities that are purely autotelic, or purely exotelic. Many professional athletes and musicians no longer enjoy much what they do, their primary motivation being their contract and paycheck. In contrast, many people do genuinely enjoy their work and would continue to be involved with it even if they were no longer paid. The important point to stress here is that although we may be paid to do something, it does not mean we cannot enjoy it, too. The surgeons we interviewed were well paid, and by and large loved what they were doing. Those who did not, were beginning to find themselves in trouble: Lacking flow in their work they sought it elsewhere, to the detriment of their professional skills and their lives as a whole.

There is no better summary of what it means to have an

autotelic attitude than this lyrical description from a young man who had a double dose of the flow experience, being both a climber and a poet:

> The mystique of rock climbing is climbing; you get to the top of a rock glad it's over but really wish it would go forever. The justification of climbing is climbing, like the justification of writing is writing . . . the act of writing justifies poetry. Climbing is the same: recognizing that you are a flow. The purpose of the flow is to keep on flowing, not looking for a peak or utopia but staying in the flow. It is not a moving up but a continuous flowing; you move up only to keep the flow going.

"Granted," a skeptic might at this point argue, "this doing something for its own sake makes some sense when one is playing, climbing, writing poetry, or making music. But what relevance can it possibly have for real life, where one has to work hard in an often hostile environment—on the job, for instance?"

If most of the examples of flow that have been presented in this chapter came from poets or from individuals engaged in what we usually think of as "leisure" activities, it is simply because in their accounts one can perceive most clearly the qualities of the flow experience. Art, sports, and leisure in general exist only because they are enjoyable. In that sense they are almost "pure" examples of flow, uncontaminated by other motives. But some of the testimonies included came from individuals engaged in the familiar struggles of everyday life, whether surgeons dealing with matters of life and death, workers, or mothers caring for their children. It is a mistake to conclude that flow occurs only when there is little at stake, when one is engaged in a freely chosen, exciting activity that has no real-life consequences. To fully appreciate the value of flow one must realize that *anything* can be enjoyable if the elements of flow are present—even, as we have seen, pacing back and forth in one's prison cell. Within that framework, doing a seemingly boring job can be a source of greater fulfillment than one ever thought possible.

The Origins of Flow

Flow is not a phenomenon that was discovered only recently. Although the methods of modern psychology have helped to bring it to light in a more systematic and accessible way, its fundamental aspects have long been recognized. For example more than a century ago Tolstoy gave a wonderfully accurate account of a flow experience in *Anna Karenina*, while describing how the wealthy landowner Levin learns to mow hay with a scythe, following in the steps of his serf, Titus. The passage is so vivid that it bears repeating:

> "I will swing less with my arm and more with my body," he thought, comparing Titus's row, which looked as if it had been cut with a line, with his own unevenly and irregularly scattered grass.
>
> . . . He thought of nothing, wished for nothing but not to be left behind the peasants, and to do his work as well as possible. He heard nothing but the swish of scythes, and saw before him Titus's upright figure moving away . . .
>
> Levin lost all sense of time, and could not have told whether it was late or early now. A change began to come over his work, which gave him immense satisfaction. In the midst of his toil there were moments during which he forgot what he was doing, and it came easy to him, and at those moments his row was almost as smooth and well-cut as Titus's. But as soon as he recollected what he was doing, and began trying to do better, he was at once conscious of the difficulty of his task, and the row was badly mown . . .
>
> More and more often now came those moments of

unconsciousness, when it was possible not to think of what one was doing. The scythe cut by itself. These were happy moments.

Before Tolstoy, almost all of the world's religions that sought to improve the human condition had discovered their own version of flow, and tried to make it a part of their practice, whether through ritual, prayer, or methods of inner discipline. One can find elements of the flow experience in the strict discipline of early Protestantism, in the rules of the Jesuits, and in the earlier Christian monastic orders like the Benedictines. They are even easier to recognize in Buddhism and Taoism, or in the instructions the god Shiva gave to Arjuna in the *Bhagavad-Gita*. When the anthropologist Mel Konner was once asked in a TV interview why was it that every culture produced a religion, why every culture sought God, he answered: "It's not God—they are seeking the rapture of life, to understand what it means to be alive."

Indeed flow and religion are different faces of the same quest: to find a reason, a justification for being alive. Vital religions provide opportunities for a full immersion of the body, the mind, and the emotions in a search for spiritual unity with the cosmos. As Western cultures are turning away from religion (in the United States 55 percent of young adults between eighteen and twenty-nine years of age have a very strong belief in God, but only 10 percent do in Sweden, 11 percent in the United Kingdom, and 12 percent in France. In the same age group, the frequency of going to church at least twice a year was 32 percent, 10 percent, 4 percent, and 8 percent, respectively), the answer to what it means to be alive is sought increasingly in possessions and material well-being. While flow experiences are not a substitute for religion, they do give an intimation of what the rapture of life can be, and point toward an existence more imbued with soul. We will, accordingly, end this chapter with the reflection of one of the rock climbers:

The only religious feelings I ever have stem from the mountains. I feel that the mountains make one aware of the spiritual matters . . . I am fortunate because I can appreciate these places where you can appreciate nature, the minisculeness of man and his aspirations, which can elevate one. Spiritually, religiously I can see in many ways the same thing.

Of course, the mere act of getting to the top of a mountain does not transform a climber into a saint. Like religion itself, the outward attributes of flow are no guarantee that a person who engages in them is happy, or that his consciousness is in harmony. Some climbers are motivated by ego drives or denial, just as some surgeons operate strictly for money and power—as did many popes and Buddhist abbots in the past. What flow offers is an opportunity to improve the quality of existence; how to actually implement it in one's life will be explored in the chapters to come.

Chapter 4

Flow and Growth

A s we have seen, flow makes us feel better in the moment, enabling us to experience the remarkable potential of the body and mind fully functioning in harmony. But what makes flow an even more significant tool is its ability to improve the quality of life in the long run. To see how this process works, let us return for a moment to one of the main conditions of flow, the matched balance of challenges and skills. Whenever a person undertakes an activity—for example, playing the piano—for the first time, his skills are bound to be quite rudimentary. At the beginning he enjoys picking out a simple tune with one finger. Soon, however, merely stumbling across the keyboard is bound to become boring, at which point a number of choices are available. One can stop trying to play the piano altogether. One can remain at the low level of challenge, occasionally tickling the ivories—a relaxing, mildly enjoyable affair. Or one can invest the necessary energy to attain the next level of skill, and take on a greater challenge— playing a more complex song with both hands.

In the course of learning any new skill such choices are made over and over again. A good flow activity is one that offers a very high ceiling of opportunities for improvement—playing the piano, for example, provides almost infinite challenges. Thus it invites growth. If one wants to stay in flow, he or she must progress and learn more skills, rising to new levels of complexity.

At its most fulfilling, a career in business or the professions involves a series of steps in which one takes on ever greater responsibility, making it possible to experience increasing flow for many years. Even when facing retirement one can take steps to ensure that growth will continue. At the age of fifty-six, Richard Jacobsen reflects on what he plans to do for the rest of his life after a career in real estate. Like his peers, continuing to grow is the first priority:

> I don't intend to retire in the sense of stopping doing things and just sort of sitting on the back porch reading a book. My objective is going to be: Go clear through to the end, and then I'd like to go out with my boots on . . . It's really important for me to continue to learn and to have new experiences that stretch and challenge me. I like to learn new skills and have new experiences.

One will quickly grow tired of any job if its challenges remain at the same level. "Unless I have the challenge I get bored," says James Davis of New Balance. For entrepreneurs, projects like getting a start-up going, or taking a company to a new dimension of performance, provide endless opportunities to show what they are made of. It is not too far-fetched to suggest that the growth of businesses is in large part the result of their leaders' need to grow as persons. Davis reflects on how quickly one can get accustomed to a certain level of success: "Three years ago, we were doing sales of around three hundred million, and we challenged ourselves to do a billion. We'll do a billion this year. But once you're there, it doesn't mean much. But when you're doing three hundred, it's a big deal."

Says Deborah Besemer: "I love the pace. I love the way things change and change quickly and that you're always confronted with new challenges because of that pace of change. I get very excited by challenge and growth."

In an ideal situation, employees will be promoted to positions of increasing responsibility, as their skill sets gradually improve. Or, in organizations with a flat hierarchy, they will find suitable challenges horizontally. But even with the best of management's intentions, many workers find themselves spending time in occupations that do not provide a good fit to their abilities, and lack possibilities for growth. Good managers realize that one of their main tasks lies precisely in this area of the job experience: to provide increasing variety and challenge to their workers, so as to prevent their stagnation. One obvious way to do so is through the growth of the business itself. Jack Greenberg of McDonald's remarks:

> You need growth to stimulate people to keep an interest in the business, to keep them energized and to build an organization that provides opportunity that can support community effort and that makes profit—because that's what we're about.

When asked what makes his own job most meaningful and worthwhile, C. William Pollard of ServiceMaster answers:

> For me, it has been clearly the whole process of the development of the person. And that is what has brought meaning to my work. I've seen people grow as individuals, grow in who they're becoming as well as what they're doing, grow as parents, grow as contributors in their community or contributors in their churches or places of worship, grow as healthy citizens. All those things are fulfilling to me and bring meaning to the fact that work results in that. What other activity could I be involved with where so many people had an opportunity to produce something, to achieve a result, and in all that, to also develop as persons?

And Robert Shapiro, then CEO of Monsanto, explains what he is most proud to have accomplished in his career:

> I think some people—and I think it's not just a few
> people—have a more expansive sense of their own pos-
> sibilities and of the possibilities of working with others.
> That's about it. I think that's the best thing I've done.

It's highly likely that employees who sense that their boss
defines "the best thing" he or she has accomplished as expanding their own potential will be more productive and loyal. But
one can even enjoy a job in which one has been stuck for a while,
by trying to do that job better and better—faster, more efficiently,
or more beautifully. Ultimately, each person has a significant degree of control over how many challenges she deals with. Even
the simplest task, if carried out with care and attention, can reveal
layers and layers of opportunities to hone one's skills. The same
is true of both business and personal relationships: coworkers,
friends, spouses, parents, and children can become routine unless one finds ways to deepen the emotional and mental ties.
Only a relationship that develops and matures stays fresh and
enjoyable.

The Dynamics of Flow

Figure 1 shows how a typical activity may increase in complexity
over time. Let's say that *A* represents the situation of the beginning piano player. His skills are basic, and as he slowly figures out
tunes on the keyboard he may experience some mild enjoyment.
But as his skills improve, boredom sets in *(B)* for it's no longer satisfying to play simple pieces repeatedly. At that point new opportunities arise: To learn to play better, or to choose a more difficult
piece *(C)*, which makes playing involving again. But if the level
of skill keeps increasing, boredom will set in again *(D)*, which
means that to keep enjoying the piano, even higher challenges will
have to be found *(E)*. Alternatively, this process can also lead
through the region of anxiety, as when the beginner is asked to
play a piece that is too difficult. The challenges are suddenly too

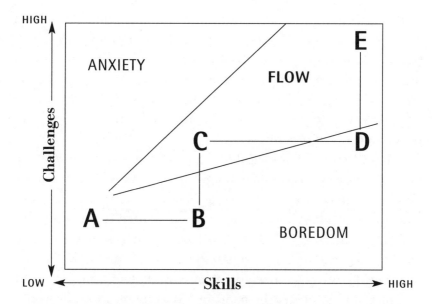

Figure 1: Growth of Complexity Through Flow. The flow experience occurs when both skills and challenges are high. A typical activity starts at A, with low challenges and skills. If one perseveres the skills will increase and the activity becomes boring(B). At that point, one will have to increase the challenges to return to flow (C). This cycle is repeated at higher levels of complexity through D and E. In a good flow activity these cycles can continue almost indefinitely.

high, and the only way to return to flow is to increase skills quickly to match. In either case, the result is the same: The individual moves to a plane of higher complexity.

Why Should Complexity Matter?

Perhaps this is a good place to examine in greater detail a term that was introduced in Chapter 2. For many people "complexity" has bad connotations, for it seems to refer to things that are complicated or cumbersome. In fact, complex systems tend to function without strain. Think of how an athlete or a violinist feels when he is in flow: He is doing something that is objectively extremely difficult, but to him it feels almost effortless.

Biology was the first of the sciences to find complexity a useful concept. Evolutionary biologists observed that over time organisms become more differentiated—they have increasingly specialized organs—and at the same time they become more integrated—the constituent parts work better together. For this reason, many have argued that evolution is primarily concerned with the increase in the complexity of organisms.

But it is not only biological forms that tend to grow more complex. The same is true of man-made objects. Think of how a photographic camera worked fifty years ago, when it was a simple machine with a lens and a shutter. If one wanted to use it indoors one had to attach a flash to it; to shoot a distant object a telephoto lens had to be added; to estimate the best aperture of the lens a handheld light meter had to be employed. The film had to be threaded and advanced by hand in a darkroom. In other words, the simple machine was very complicated to use. Now we have a complex machine that is very simple to use: All the functions of the flash, the telephoto, the light meter, and so on have been built into the camera; the photographer has but to aim and shoot.

This is a paradigm of the process that makes life more civilized, more comfortable over time. Everything from textiles to weapons, from homes to meals becomes more complex: more difficult to make, but easier to use. Just as without an uninterrupted line of biological ancestors our bodies wouldn't have developed to their current state, so, too, we wouldn't have commodities like woven clothes or TV dinners without an uninterrupted line of knowledge transmitted through the culture from one generation to the next. The evolution of culture is based on the differentiation and integration of earlier artifacts and previous knowledge. This process of transmission means we don't have to reinvent the wheel every generation, needlessly wasting precious mental resources in the process.

Groups of people can also be described as being more or less complex. A crowd is neither differentiated nor integrated; a bureaucracy is usually the latter but not the former. Is the typical de-

partment that is run along "command-and-control" lines a complex system? Probably not, because by not utilizing the employees'
unique skills it is not very differentiated. It may be well integrated
in that everyone knows his duties and collaborates smoothly, but
maintaining order in such a system is both costly and inefficient,
because the employees would not work spontaneously toward the
same goals without management's constant efforts to keep them
in line. However, a very laissez-faire organization would not be complex, either. It may be differentiated, but its components would
not fit well with one another or work together seamlessly. Again,
one of the key tasks of management is to create an organization
that stimulates the complexity of those who belong to it.

We have seen in Chapter 2 that complexity is the central feature of personal development. As the years pass, physical and
mental maturation provide new skills to the individual, and society
expects increasingly productive and responsible behavior. Many
people go through life never quite finding a way to match their
talents to what is expected of them. They feel either that life is
passing them by—marooned in loneliness, their talents remain
useless or undeveloped—or that they are being crushed by excessive demands from relatives and bosses, never able to find time for
themselves.

Those who are able to find the middle way weave opportunities
and abilities together in an enjoyable progress toward complexity.
Our research shows that teenagers who are in flow more often develop more productive habits: Not only are they much happier
and more optimistic, and have higher self-esteem, but they study
more, are involved in active leisure more often, and spend more
time with friends—a finding that is independent of income,
parental education, and social status. Adults who are more often
in flow are not only happier, but they spend significantly more
time at work actually working instead of gossiping, reading the papers, or surfing the Web.

Children's ability to experience flow is made possible in part by
having access to *social capital*—the infrastructure that is in place to

make life less daunting. When parents and schools invest energy in them, children are more likely to get started on the path of complexity. Teens who experience flow most often typically come from families that are both more demanding and more support-ive. That is, they are more complex. These young people spend more time with adults, have access to more books (but not neces-sarily to computers or other appliances), and come from schools that have a stronger school spirit.

For adults, perhaps the most important source of social capital is the job. To the extent that they can feel challenged and sup-ported at work, that there is variety and increasing opportunities to learn and to use one's capacity to its fullest, flow is likely to oc-cur. In fact, variety on the job, and the support of a supervisor are the most often cited reasons for workers' satisfaction.

Lacking these conditions, work inevitably becomes a source of alienation and apathy. When Masaru Ibuka started Sony in 1945—before he had any capital, profits, or promising product—he wrote a mission statement that listed as the first " Purposes of In-corporation" of his company the following item:

> To establish a place of work where engineers can feel
> the joy of technological innovation, be aware of their
> mission to society, and work to their heart's content.

Working with joy to one's heart's content while responding to society's needs is a perfect description of how flow functions in the workplace. It seems that the half century of success that Sony has enjoyed is to no small extent due to the fact that Ibuka's vision was actually implemented there, and has been made a priority ever since.

How Happiness Fluctuates Across the Day

If one wants to make it possible for the employees of one's organi-zation to work "to their hearts' content," it is useful to consider the ebb and flow of their moods, and the causes of them. No person can be in flow all the time; periods of stress, boredom, and occasional despair shadow everyone's consciousness.

In the studies I have conducted since the mid-1970s, I set out to measure the quality of experience people report at various moments in their lives. The experience sampling method, as I called this procedure, involves volunteers' carrying for a week a programmable watch (or other signaling devices, like a Palm Pilot) that will alert them eight to ten times a day at random moments. At each signal they write down where they are, what they are doing, and what they are thinking about. Then they rate along a series of numerical scales their mood, self-esteem, concentration—and also the level of challenges they were encountering and skills they were using at the moment of the signal. Each subject thus provides about fifty data points for each one of the thirty to fifty responses they give during the week. If all the data collected by our team and by other universities around the world were merged, there would be well over a quarter million responses to analyze. What follows in this section has been compiled from this enormous database collected over the past decades.

Figure 2 is a schematic summary of how our feelings change as a result of different combinations of opportunities to act, or challenges, on the one hand, and the availability of personal capacities, or skills, on the other. The central point in Figure 2 represents the subjects' average level of challenges and skills throughout the week of testing. The closer people are to this central point, the more average their moods tend to be—neither positive nor negative. But as their scores move away from this central point, distinct states of mind begin to emerge depending on the ratio of challenges to skills.

Basically, the more a person feels skilled, the more her moods will improve; while the more challenges that are present, the more her attention will become focused and concentrated. As we would expect, optimal experience is represented by the flow "channel," where both challenges and skills lie above the average

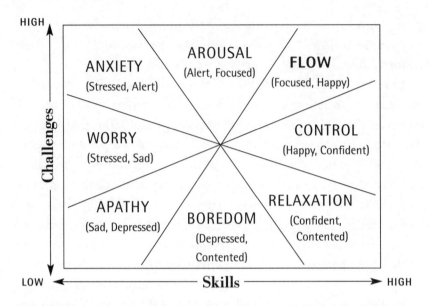

Figure 2: The Map of Everyday Experience. When people perceive themselves to be above their own personal average level of challenges and skills, they experience flow. The opposite is the state of apathy, where both challenges and skills are low. Other combinations of challenges and skills produce feelings of worry, anxiety, and arousal (when challenges outweigh skills), or control, relaxation, and boredom (when skills outweigh challenges). Some of the other prominent emotions typical of each "channel" are indicated in parentheses.

level—at such moments, one is both happy and focused. This is the condition the poet and the athlete, the surgeon and the mountaineer describe when they are at the peak of their experience. In the other seven "channels" challenges and skills are not so high and in balance, and either happiness or concentration, or both, weaken.

Two other channels are associated with positive emotions. The first is the one labeled "arousal," where due to slightly higher challenges a person must concentrate but does not feel quite at ease. In this situation, if one wants to enter flow, the level of skills must be improved. Because flow is so attractive, a person in arousal is likely to be motivated to reach that state, and thus learns and grows to accomplish that. The other positive channel is "control," where skills slightly outweigh challenges. This is a perfectly comfortable place in which to be, and some people are happiest in this condition. But because it does not require high concentration one does not operate at 100 percent capacity, and so it is not as enjoyable as flow. However, it is relatively easy to move from this condition into flow, by choosing somewhat higher challenges. Arousal and control are both states that lead easily to learning because they stimulate us to develop higher complexity.

The remaining possibilities grow progressively worse. "Relaxation" is still reasonably positive, but "boredom" and especially "apathy" fail to be engaging, resulting in feelings of sadness and listlessness. One gets the sense that life is passing by, with associated loneliness and helplessness. Of all these states "anxiety" is the one people try to avoid the most. Even though in some respects it is better than "apathy," which leads nowhere, "anxiety" may spur one to take charge of a situation. All too often, however, an anxious person will despair of reaching flow because the gap between skills and challenges seems insurmountable. If this is the case, instead of remaining in a state of anxiety, one is likely to escape the situation by reducing challenges and falling into worry or apathy. This can be accomplished in several ways: by giving up responsibilities, by scaling down ambitions, or by denying reality. If all else fails it can be achieved by chemical means: Through drugs or alcohol one can forget temporarily that there are pressing tasks requiring action.

Of course humans experience a great variety of other emotions not represented in this model, from surprise to rage, from impatience to jealousy, just to name a few. However, these eight provide a serviceable compass by which to find one's way through the thickets of emotional life. The direction toward which the model clearly points is flow: If we can create situations where people's skills are engaged by progressively higher challenges, we can expect the quality of life to improve, and complexity to increase.

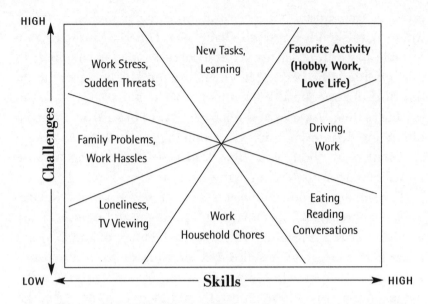

Figure 3: The Relation of Activities to the Quality of Experience. Some daily activities are likely to produce flow, while others are more likely to lead to anxiety, or relaxation. Figure 3 shows some of the typical activities associated with different combinations of challenges and skills, and hence with different emotions (see also Figure 2). Note that in a work situation one can either be in flow, in control, bored, worried, or anxious, depending on the ratio of challenges to skills.

The eight combinations of challenges and skills usually occur as the person is involved in different activities. Figure 3 shows some of the typical combinations of activity and the associated emotion. As one would expect, flow is experienced most often when someone is doing what he likes best—which, of course, will differ for different people. For some it will be sports; for others, music or art. One interesting (and reassuring) finding is that when driving a car, people are most often in the control channel, provided they are not stuck in a traffic jam, in which case they would be in boredom or apathy; or provided that there is no sudden snowstorm, in which case they are likely to be in anxiety. While a great many people do find flow in work, it can, of course, also produce anxiety, apathy, or boredom, depending on how skills and challenges are aligned.

Many different activities provide relaxation: eating, napping, socializing with friends, and a variety of leisure pursuits. Boredom, while usually associated with maintenance functions like cleaning the house, shopping for groceries, or mowing the yard, is all too often the mental state most prevalent at work. Apathy, which occurs when there is nothing to do, is such an intolerable state that to avoid it people resort to the most readily available means of escape, which often turns out to be a passive leisure activity, such as watching television.

Worry and anxiety are caused by threats that we feel are progressively beyond our control. They may include major catastrophes like war, economic depression, or neighborhood crime, but are typically caused by more immediate stressful events, such as the illness of a child, the strains in a marriage, or one's own inadequacy. Such experiences are also not uncommon on the job. People often feel most worried when their work is not going well, and most anxious when dealing with their bosses.

Clearly, it would be impossible to be in flow all the time, for the rhythms of life do not allow it. We have to rest, to spend time doing unglamorous tasks like mopping the floor or taking showers. We need to relax. There will always be threats that place us in jeopardy. Nevertheless, there is also enormous room for improvement in how often we can access flow. According to surveys conducted by the Gallup Organization in the United States and similar firms in Europe, between 15 percent and 20 percent of adults never seem to experience flow, while a comparable number claim to experience it every day. The other 60 percent to 70 percent report being intensely involved in what they do anywhere from once every few months to at least once a week. This disparity is a telling indication of how great a possibility exists for raising the quality of life overall and presents a tremendous opportunity for managers who are committed to enhancing joy and innovation in their workplaces.

The Building of Psychological Capital

A single episode of flow lifts the spirit momentarily; when experienced over time, flow helps make a person unique and indispensable. It is useful to think of enjoyment as the psychological
equivalent of building capital, and of pleasure as the equivalent of
consumption. As used in economics the term "capital" would be
defined as follows: *Capital refers to resources withheld from immediate
consumption in the expectation of greater future returns.* However con-
troversial a topic it has been, capital has been the main—if not the
only—way of achieving progress, even in violently anticapitalist,
socialist countries. A dam, a hospital, a university, a cathedral, or a
national park cannot be built without using up resources that
would be easier to consume immediately, and none of them would
be built at all unless they were believed to provide some greater
returns in the future. The "returns" from a park, a church, or a
dam are, of course, very different from one another, but they are
all expected to contribute to a better quality of life.

In our own lives consider the kind of choice most of us confront every day upon coming home from work: Do we sit down to
read a stimulating book (taking a bike ride, playing the guitar, vol-
unteering at the hospital, and so on, could be substituted for reading), or do we drop in front of the TV? Most people would agree
that watching television would be the more pleasant choice, for it
would be easier, more relaxing, and more hassle-free. But which
choice would ultimately be more enjoyable? Which would contribute more to happiness in the long run? Again, most people
would probably say the first one. And they would be correct.

But what, precisely, is the resource being "consumed" during
the more pleasant activity, and "withdrawn from consumption"
when we are involved in the more enjoyable one? At the psychological level, the most basic resource involved is attention. Attention is the brain's capacity to process information, and to direct
action. It is a limited resource, because we cannot process more

than a few bits of information at any single moment, and thus we can only be aware of a tiny fraction of what is going on inside us or around us. Attention is *psychic energy*, and like physical energy, unless we allocate some part of it to the task at hand, no work gets done.

If you doubt the truth of this principle, just try to read this book while playing the piano, or to balance the checkbook and drive the car at the same time (on second thought, better not try this one). Or try to have a meaningful conversation with your child while thinking about a problem on the job. Each of these simple tasks becomes impossible to do in combination, due to the narrow range of stimuli our brain can deal with concurrently.

Thus one of the fashionable concepts of high-tech companies, "multitasking," is more a myth than a reality. Humans cannot really successfully multitask, but can rather move attention rapidly from one task to the other in quick succession, which only makes us feel as if we were actually doing things simultaneously. However, this strategy is not as effective as is widely believed. It takes anywhere from fifteen minutes to an hour to get one's mind around a difficult problem, to establish the conditions to develop a worthwhile solution. If one switches too soon and too often from one task to the next, it is likely that what the mind will come up with is going to be superficial, if not trivial. It is much preferable to work on a single task until one becomes stymied; at that point switching to another problem will come as a relief. Then, after the new task becomes tiresome, one can return to the original problem refreshed.

In knowledge-intensive business settings, where every manager has to oversee massive amounts of information as well as people, facilitating the use of psychic energy becomes a primary concern. In such firms it is true that "the scarcest resource is attention," yet far too much of this resource is mismanaged and wasted because we have no idea how to deal with it effectively.

It is actually possible to estimate how much psychic energy each of us may have in an average lifespan of seventy-five years.

The brain can process on the order of 110 bits of information each second (To understand what another person is saying to us, for example, requires about forty bits, which explains why we cannot understand more than two people talking at the same time.) Thus the limit of what we can experience in a lifetime, assuming we are awake sixteen hours each day and live to be seventy-five, is roughly 173 *billion* bits of information. While this is an impressively large figure, when one begins to consider the amount of psychic energy it takes merely to get ready in the morning, eat breakfast, drive to work, and so on, not much of it is left for substantive purposes.

Yet every experience we have—every thought, feeling, desire, or memory; every act, conversation, or accomplishment—must pass through the screen of attention for it to become real to us, and thus must be accounted for by some portion of those 173 billion bits. What we call our life is the sum of all the experiences that have filtered through attention over time. From this perspective, it is easy to understand that what we pay attention to, and how we pay attention, determine the content and quality of life.

Psychic energy is consumed when the attention we invest does not produce any change in the mind—when no lasting memories are laid down, no new skills develop, no relationships are strengthened. When a person uses up a fraction of his life and nothing complex results from it, he is wasting psychic energy. By contrast psychological capital is built up when the attention invested results in a more complex consciousness—more refined skills, a fuller understanding of some subject, a deeper relationship. This usually takes place when we use our skills to confront a higher level of challenges—in other words, when we experience flow. These are the kind of investments of attention that will bring returns later in the form of an improved quality of life.

Any activity that is complex is more rare and difficult to achieve than a comparable activity in a simpler form. For instance there are fewer pianists who can play Rachmaninoff's third piano concerto well than there are who can play his second, for the third is a more technically challenging piece that requires greater skills. To develop such a skill requires a large investment of attention not only on the part of the student but also on the part of society: Teachers, mentors, prizes, concert stages must be available to nurture the young pianist to higher levels of perfection. In other words, social capital must be invested in building psychological capital.

Similarly, fewer jumpers can clear a bar set at six feet than at five, and fewer still can clear the bar at seven feet. Each inch increase in height reflects a more complex performance, one that is rarer because fewer people are born with the physique to do it, and one that requires more time and effort to master. Each inch demands not only a greater investment of psychic energy, a larger slice out of one's life, but also a greater commitment of social capital in the form of coaching, equipment, travel, and so on. Complexity does not come cheap; anything outstanding and enduring has its costs, either material or psychological.

It is for this reason that people who learn to invest psychic energy in complex activities have the opportunity to become more complex themselves. It would be easy to misunderstand this point as advocating the old notion of "postponing gratification"—that is, if you spend a lot of time working hard and being miserable, you'll eventually be rewarded. This is, in fact, the opposite of what our research shows. What we have found is that young people who are learning a challenging, hard-working lifestyle are happier and more satisfied with what they are doing. It is those who choose pleasure over enjoyment—who spend all their free time hanging out and watching TV—who are sad, listless, and anxious.

Yet one intriguing bit of evidence does seem to give credence to the view of hard work as "postponement of gratification." Engaged young people—those who are in flow more often and undertake more challenging tasks—also say: "I wish I was doing something else" more than the disengaged ones. In other words, even though they are happier, more involved, and are progressing toward a more gratifying future, they still wish they could be doing low-energy, pleasurable things like going to the mall or the beach rather than the demanding, enjoyable ones like studying or practicing the flute. We found a similar trend, one not as strong but still quite significant, in adults.

How can this paradox be explained? Why is it that people would rather not do what makes them happy, both in the present and in the long run? There are two likely reasons for this attitude—both of which are in our power to change. The first is that our culture generally endorses pleasure over enjoyment, and for an obvious reason: Pleasure is more profitable. Most advertising is dedicated to convincing us that we will be happier buying the latest products. An individual who goes against the grain and instead chooses to build psychological capital becomes a less avid consumer. If one compares Asian American teens with Caucasian Americans, for example, one discovers that the former are more likely to experience flow from challenging activities. Even though they also live in the United States, Asian cultural beliefs are still strong enough within their families to make them accept that learning can be enjoyable.

It is true that flow requires more effort than pleasure, for as we have argued earlier, enjoyment depends on investments of psychic energy. The mistake is in believing that the experience of effort itself is worse than that of pleasure. On the elaborate wooden gate leading to the school in the village from which my family comes, in darkest Transylvania, there are some runes carved that, when translated from Hungarian, state: "The roots of knowledge are bitter, but its fruits are sweet." Unfortunately it is widely believed that learning must not only be hard, but also bitter. In fact, it is the way we teach that is usually bitter, and not the learning itself.

This brings us to the second reason for the paradox: Many of the challenging, complex activities we must undertake in everyday life are so badly designed that instead of producing flow, they produce anxiety or boredom. It is true that learning for its own sake is typically enjoyable, but can the same be said of *school* learning? The assembly-line methods commonly applied to education all too often produce neither joy nor learning. The same is true of work: While most people enjoy working when it provides flow, too few jobs are so designed as to make flow possible.

This is where management can make a real difference. While not even the most gifted leader can force her workers to enjoy and grow on their jobs, there is a great deal that even an average manager can do to make the workplace more amenable to flow. If one truly cares about the bottom line in the broadest sense of that term, the first priority is to eliminate obstacles to flow at all levels of the firm and to substitute practices and policies that are designed to make work enjoyable. In the next chapter we shall consider ideas about how to make that possible.

Growing Throughout Life

People who rise to positions of leadership in business—or for that matter, in other walks of life, as well—do not depend on the support of the environment for their growth. Or more accurately, they are proactive and seek out whatever support they need, wherever they can find it. They are so determined to learn, to change, and to shape their experiences that whatever the situation in which they find themselves, they will find a way to increase the complexity of their lives. Of course, their needs change through time, and what they require at age thirty is different from what is necessary at fifty or seventy. The Body Shop's Anita Roddick reflects on having reached middle age:

> The notion at the moment for my life and in my work is reflection. It's collating stories, gathering the stories, which I think are a great part of the wisdom and the myths and legends of your life, or your business life, or your relationship life. . . . [It's] huge fun [that] this gaggle of grandchildren coming into my life should have calmed me down and made me a little less peripatetic—you know, all over the place. So it's a charmed time. . . . I found ways around this new stage in my life and the

company, which is almost setting up a skunk works—a group of creative, wild, counter-culture people, who even though they're funded by the company, are not that part of the system. So we're creating wild ideas, and we just plop them into the company. Because we're free. We're braver visually or we're braver with words. And it's a joy. . . . Life is really exciting. I haven't gone through a period in my life when I've thought back and thought, "Oh God, this is not what I want."

"Fun," "charmed time," "free," "joy,"—notice the words Anita chooses to describe her experience. Clearly flow is an integral part of her days, as it is of virtually all the visionary leaders we interviewed. If the challenges of their jobs become exhausted, they find new ones: Most of our subjects dedicated increasing amounts of time to community improvement, philanthropy, family, active hobbies, travel, reflection, and spirituality. In a way, they can afford to do so, for they have had their successes and have made their millions. But the reason they can go on enjoying life is not because they are rich and comfortable, but because they are actively seeking new challenges and developing new skills, and thus unfolding their being along increasingly complex lines.

Part II

Flow and Organizations

Chapter 5

Why Flow Doesn't Happen on the Job

T he goal of management is to create value through the labor of people working together for a common cause. There are many ways to accomplish this, including slavery and bribery, but here we shall focus on the best way to manage people, which is to create an environment where employees actually enjoy their work and grow in the process of doing it. From the viewpoint of the firm such a workplace is ideal because it attracts the most able individuals, is likely to keep them longer, and obtains spontaneous effort from their work. It is best, too, from the viewpoint of employees, because it helps them to a happier life, and it supports the development of their personal complexity. First, however, it will be useful to consider what motivates people to work, and the various forms that work can take.

In a sense, it should not be difficult to get people working, because our bodies are built for just such a purpose. The human nervous system functions best when challenged, when focused on a task; most of us feel best about ourselves after a job well done. And yet anyone who has been in charge of employees knows how problematic it is to get consistently good work out of a group of people. Why this contradiction?

Certainly one explanation is that while people are built to work, most jobs are not built for people. What employers from the pharaohs down to modern TQM managers have been primarily concerned about is not how to tailor a job so as to bring out the best in the workers, but rather how to get the *most* out of them. So one of the intriguing paradoxes of the human condition is that while surveys indicate that about 80 percent of adults claim that they would continue to work even if they had so much money that they didn't have to worry about having more, the majority can hardly wait each day to leave their job and go home. It seems that one could say about work what is asserted about the opposite sex: "You can't live with it, and you can't live without it."

The challenge for someone who wants to create an environment that attracts and retains enthusiastic and enterprising workers is to understand why people want to work in the first place, and then provide the conditions that fulfill that need. This is especially true in rapidly changing times, when knowledge workers are searching for jobs that will expand their opportunities most fully. The manager who can provide an environment conducive to growth will have access to this indispensable human capital.

How we experience work is determined by three conditions. The first is what kind of job happens to be available. The same word—"work"—describes a range of occupations, from what a banker does in his mahogany-paneled suite, to what the ditch-digger does under the beating sun. Some ways of making a living are inherently enjoyable, while others can be numbingly inhuman. Working conditions can also change over time—at one point the work week may last eighty hours, and at another only half as long. The objective conditions of the workplace will therefore determine to a great extent whether people will be motivated to work or not.

The second factor involves the values attached to labor, the interpretations a culture provides for working. Sometimes the messages are contradictory: The Bible teaches us that work is a punishment visited on humankind because of Adam's presumption, but then the "Protestant ethic" suggests that work is the path to salvation. The Dilbert cartoons portray office work as a mindless charade run by evil morons, but at the same time unemployment is viewed as almost a form of social disease. In a way it is not surprising that feelings about work are so ambivalent, because some jobs are undeniably meaningless and brutish, whereas others are challenging and rewarding. Yet any job becomes more attractive if it is considered meaningful by society. For instance, the sixth most frequently mentioned job that American teenagers state they would like to have when they grow up is teaching, even though they know it involves hard work and low pay, because the job is seen as one that adds value to individual lives and to the community.

And last but not least, whether one is motivated to work or not depends on the attitude one has toward one's job. For no matter how uninspiring that job may be, it is possible to find redeeming value in it if one knows what to look for. Poets enthuse about being able to see a world in a grain of sand, and holding infinity in one's palm. In fact there are assembly-line workers and dishwashers who regard their menial jobs as rich drama, and relish doing them. On the other hand, many a well-paid professional or CEO hates his potentially exciting job, and looks for ways to get out of it as soon as possible.

Thus a manager who wants to build an organization that will last, one in which people are motivated to contribute and to stay, has these three options. The first is to make the objective conditions of the workplace as attractive as possible. The second is to find ways to imbue the job with meaning and value. Third, by selecting and rewarding individuals who find satisfaction in their work, leaders can steer the morale of the organization as a whole in a positive direction. In an ideal case, all three of these steps will be taken. The rest of this book will explore specific ways to create such enduring organizations. But first, to understand better how work actually fits in people's lives, a brief historical detour may be useful. If all we know is what we experience in the present, we will have only a partial, distorted view. To truly understand what work in our own time means, we must compare it to the many different ways people made a living in other times, in other places.

The Changing Conditions of Work

To survive, every living thing must give up some of its energy in the hope of getting more energy back with which to grow and reproduce. In this most general sense, work is what an organism does to keep entropy from breaking it down. The cougar must expend energy in the form of running to overtake the deer, and if it's lucky, the meal will provide more calories than what had been lost in the chase. Humans have devised a great variety of ways to obtain the necessary calories. In earliest times, all humans were hunter-gatherers; like the cougar, they fed on animal proteins, and perhaps even more on roots and berries usually collected by women. For many hundreds of thousands of years, these were such natural behaviors that they didn't feel at all like what we are used to calling "work."

Extrapolating from what anthropologists have learned about contemporary peoples whose lifestyle is based on a similar subsistence economy, our ancestors may not have "worked" more than two to three hours a day. Such labor was simply an accepted part of life and it would have made no sense for them to have thought of these activities as distinct from leisure. And in fact, our ancestors didn't have leisure as such, either—they filled their free time with meaningful, necessary activities like visiting relatives, carving tools, and dancing in the ceremonies that kept their world on an even keel. We can only guess, but judging from the surviving cultures that are still close to this way of living, it is likely that flow was not difficult to achieve, because there were few social constraints keeping a person from doing what she could do. Each used whatever skills he or she had, goals were clear, and feedback was immediate.

In the hunting-gathering economy it was impossible for one person to exploit the work of another. For most of human history, almost no surplus was produced. Since they had to be constantly on the move, people could not afford to accumulate possessions. No individual was wealthier than another, or could pay another to do a job. In that sense our ancestors were independent producers, closer to the freelance professionals and knowledge workers of our times than to any workers in the intervening millennia. But in another sense hunter-gatherers were extremely *inter*dependent, for most goods were shared in the family, the kin group, or the tribe as a whole. Property was communal rather than personal.

In describing the practices of Australian aborigines, anthropologists report that if after a tiring but successful hunt a man brought home a kangaroo, he would never consider keeping the meat just for himself and his immediate family. Instead he would cut up the carcass and, following ancient customs, would give the left hind leg to his brother, the tail to his father's brother's son, the loins and fat to his father-in-law, the ribs to his mother-in-law, and so on, keeping for himself only the entrails and the blood—tasty, no doubt, but certainly not the choice parts of the animal. To share the spoils this way was like buying an insurance policy; sooner or later one would collect from the relatives who had benefited from one's contributions. (In any case, if a hunter had kept the entire kangaroo for himself, in a few days he'd have been left with only a pile of maggoty meat.)

While for most of human history people didn't "work" in the modern sense, even today there are still a few individuals—usually among artists, writers, scientists, inventors, and entrepreneurs—who choose when and how to work and control what they do. They claim that it is equally true that they never worked a day in their lives as it is to say that they worked every minute of their lives. They are at their jobs while in the shower, while driving the car, while making spaghetti sauce; their minds are constantly struggling with problems, turning them around, examining them from new angles. But to them, this intense activity feels as effortless as breathing. John Hope Franklin, a leading African American historian, admitted sheepishly, "Come Friday, I also say 'TGIF'— thank God it's Friday—because then I look forward to two uninterrupted days of work at home."

George Klein, a biologist who studies tumors and cancers at the

Karolinska Institute in Stockholm, is almost always in flow, or in his words, he experiences "the happiness of a deer running through a meadow." He dislikes small talk, parties, idle social encounters, anything that interferes with his research. One recent evening all of his colleagues left the lab for a picnic celebration of Midsummer's Eve, a major holiday in Sweden. Desperate to avoid what he feared would be a boring social ritual, Klein found an excuse to remain in the laboratory alone. To keep himself busy he decided to carry out a delicate procedure that was usually performed by his assistants, who were away at the party. It turned out that he was completely inept at this task, and ended up destroying some rare tumor specimens of Burkitt's lymphoma that he had just received from Africa. Yet Klein kept being cheerful throughout the long night:

> I remained into the wee hours studying tube after tube and could only confirm that everything was spoiled. At four in the morning I admitted total defeat and gave up. I was in a total state of euphoria. While driving home that bright Midsummer's morning, I wondered how I could be so happy after having destroyed the excellent samples. The answer was obvious: I had been excused from participating in the Midsummer's dance.

For scientists, artists, and entrepreneurs—knowledge workers who set their own goals and their own pace—what they do for a living is so much a part of who they are that to call it "work" is merely a social convention.

For the majority of humanity, however, things changed rather abruptly about ten thousand years ago, when farming was discovered and proved to be a more efficient and dependable way to provide calories than the nomadic lifestyle of hunter-gatherers. For the first time, a few individuals were able to accumulate surplus food, and with it possessed the resources to hire others to do their bidding. Instead of having to roam across the landscape in search of nutrition, farmers could settle in villages and then cities, accumulating property. It was agriculture that made the division of labor possible, and thus created the conditions for civilized (that is "cityfied") living. The downside has been that it also made possible the exploitation of labor, which contributed to the negative connotations associated with work.

This pattern has repeated itself throughout history whenever a new technological development has allowed some enterprising individuals to get an edge over the rest of the population. It happened again in the Middle Ages when a few knights arrayed in expensive armor were able to force defenseless farmers to share their produce. It happened when the first factories using mechanical looms put thousands of independent cottage industries out of business, and then hired the unemployed weavers as factory hands. In each case, a minority who happened to be well positioned to exploit the new way of doing things was able to benefit, and as a result opened a wide gap in the ownership of resources. The minority in power then used political and legal means to institutionalize and protect its predominance—until a new political or technological revolution came along to challenge entrenched inequalities.

The latest turn of this pattern is now taking place in the United States, as the government has been co-opted to protect the gains of the few who were able to benefit from recent technological advances. Through changes in tax and inheritance laws the gap between the very rich and the poor keeps growing wider. Less than a generation ago, Americans would smugly look down on countries like Brazil for the huge disparities that existed there between the wealthiest sectors of the economy and the widespread poverty. Few could have imagined then that by the turn of the century the world's largest gap in income would be in the United States, causing an increasing sense of vulnerability among those who already felt threatened in their livelihood. For workers scrambling to keep their foothold yet falling back two steps for each step forward, their jobs, instead of being the joyful expression of their beings, become a hated necessity.

Even this exceedingly compressed history suggests that working has been a very varied experience, ranging from being a source of deep flow to one of absolute misery. But what are the current conditions of work, when compared against those in the past? In the first place, the amount of time most people work nowadays falls roughly halfway between the few hours a day spent by hunter-gatherers, and the fourteen hours and more that the industrial workers had to labor in early factories. Certainly current conditions are more pleasant and more humane than they have typically been in the past. But such improvements do not guarantee that the average workers are having more flow experiences while at their jobs than they did earlier. There are several reasons for this.

In the first place, *few jobs nowadays have clear goals.* Fewer still provide goals that are also the worker's own, rather than the organization's. The Inuit hunter seeks to kill a seal because his and his family's survival depends on it—every move of the hunt derives its meaning from that simple goal. Because of this, the hunter could sit for hours with spear in hand at the edge of a hole in the ice, focusing on the most minute changes in the surface of the water, and not feel stressed or bored at the end of the day.

Much of what modern workers are required to do on the job is dictated by demands that make sense at some higher organizational level, but are obscure to the worker. Why do we need to fill out these forms? What is the purpose of this rule? What is the outcome of this process? And often even if the worker understands *what* she is doing, it is not clear to her *why.* Yet without well-defined goals, both long-term and moment by moment, it is difficult to enjoy what one is doing.

The second obstacle is that *contemporary jobs seldom provide adequate feedback.* Even when feedback is provided, a worker is often simply told, you are doing okay, but most any fool could do what you are doing—you are a replaceable cog in an impersonal machine. In the past a craftsman—whether a shoemaker, carpenter, or weaver—was able to see the object of his labors taking shape before his eyes. Each move was an expression of his skills, and it was his choice whether to do the job excellently or just passably, depending on his mood and the circumstances.

As everything from industrial production to clerical tasks has been rationalized, workers are seldom able to see how what they do is an expression of their own being. What their labor does express, rather, is a work plan designed by others, and their sole responsibility is to reproduce it more or less mechanically. So even if they do the job well, the feedback is not addressed to their own ingenuity, but largely to the plans and equipment that made it possible. It is hard to get deeply involved in an activity where one's performance is a minor factor, where a good job is scarcely noticed, and where even the worker can't determine whether his work was well done.

Lack of feedback is a problem not only for workers, but also for leadership, and the firm as a whole. In large organizations the dilution of information as it passes up and down the hierarchy, and horizontally across departments, can undermine the effort to focus on common goals. As Cambridge Incubator founder, Timothy Rowe, notes: "A lot of problems in business are not because the CEO doesn't have the right values. It's because the CEO isn't effective at communicating them throughout the entire organization." In a ten-thousand-person organization some awful stuff may happen without anyone in authority being aware of it.

In many jobs, *the skills of the worker are not well matched to the opportunities for action.* This is true even of highly paid knowledge work where, for example, well-trained young lawyers are assigned to years of monotonous library research that makes few demands on their skills beyond tolerance for boredom and the ability to put up with long hours, or where ambitious young consultants are thrown into stressful eighty-hour-a-week workloads that burn them out in a matter of years.

The specialization of functions, which has been one of the main factors in the increased efficiency of industrial production, has also had the negative effect of requiring only a limited number of a worker's skills. Even today, there are some jobs that do call upon the full range of a worker's talents. The few remaining independent farmers must learn to be economists, mechanics, veterinarians, weathermen, and all-around problem solvers if they want to prosper. In the regions of northern Italy where families of weavers still own their looms, parents and children jointly design fabrics, decide on a production schedule, buy old machines in Germany or France and then recondition them. Then they market and sell their silk patterns to buyers in Japan—as well as run a dozen or so looms each day from dawn to dusk. The children of these families learn all the relevant skills—fixing machines, designing fabrics, marketing, and selling—at their own pace, under the mentorship of their parents.

A job that employs only a fraction of one's skills quickly becomes a burden. One feels that most of one's potential is left unused, wasted. Consider the clerk at the department of transportation whose job it is to pass out forms to endless lines of applicants for a driver's license, and then quickly check each form for completeness—how much of her being is involved in this task? Or the biochemist at a large pharmaceutical company whose responsibility it is to go down endless lists of chemical compounds to be tested according to an invariant routine? As we shall see later, it is possible to find flow even in such constricted circumstances. For many people, however, the task is simply too daunting. When most of one's skills remain unengaged, involvement in the job soon falters, and it is not surprising that one begins to yearn for free time, where there is a chance to be fully alive.

Another feature of many jobs is *lack of control*—not only over the goals of the process, but over every step of the performance. A worker who feels micromanaged soon loses interest in her job. The two most often cited complaints about jobs are lack of variety, and conflicts with a supervisor. Both of these stem from a feeling that one has been reduced to a tool without choice or voice in the enterprise. Under such conditions workers will at most give only what is expected of them, but rarely more.

Almost all human groups need some form of hierarchy, a ladder of increasing responsibility and power. Every complex system has a division of labor, a specialization of functions that includes mechanisms of control. But the need for control from above must be balanced against the need for autonomy that even the humblest person holds dear. Especially destructive is the behavior of those managers who insist upon controlling others not for the benefit of the organization but to bolster their own personal quest for power. In such by no means rare cases, subordinates become unwilling to sacrifice their own lives for another person's selfish agenda, and begin to withdraw psychic energy from the job.

Finally, the fact that *the use of time is specified by rhythms external to the worker* creates another set of constraints. The activity of hunters was dictated by the wanderings of game, and that of farmers by the changing of seasons—conditions that made perfect sense, even if they demanded long and strenuous bouts of work at the appropriate times. In the few remaining cottage industries of Europe, craftsmen still pass on their tools to their wives or children when the mushrooms sprout in the forest, or the trout start running in the river. The use of time is flexible, open to changing opportunities and the internal states of the worker.

The requirements of industrial production put an end to all that about two centuries ago. The inflexible nine-to-five schedule (which was a great improvement on the five-to-nine routine of the early decades of the Industrial Revolution) created an inflexible timeframe in which a person's psychic energy was no longer under his or her control—whether there was actually work to be done or not.

Recent advances in communication technologies however, have made both work*place* and work*time* much more relative concepts. The home computer connected by a modem to the company office makes it possible for an increasing number of workers to set their own pace. In the traditional ranching communities of western Montana a class of "modem cowboys" is developing—workers who are in daily touch with the insurance companies or marketing departments that employ them in Dallas or Kansas City. They, too, can decide to pick mushrooms or go fishing whenever they wish.

However, the spread of flextime and part-time work and telecommuting is still an option only for those who seek to find a healthier balance between work and family. Those who wish to succeed in the dominant corporate culture are still being evaluated in terms of the amount of *overtime* they are willing to invest at their workplace. While the extrinsic rewards within the organization (remuneration, advancement, power) tend to be directly proportional to the amount of time one invests in organizational goals, the intrinsic rewards (the sense of a job well done, with skill and integrity) are often inversely related. Thus stress for knowledge workers continues to climb as the amount of time at their disposal keeps shrinking. We still have a long way to go before a sensible allocation of time is in effect at most companies.

In conclusion, achieving flow at work is made difficult by obstacles that militate against the conditions necessary for flow to occur. All too often, the job fails to provide clear goals, adequate feedback, a balance of challenges and skills, a sense of control, and a flexible use of time. Considering all these obstructions, it is remarkable how often people at work are still able to experience flow. Nevertheless, redesigning the workplace promises to lead to an enormous improvement in the "bottom line" of human happiness.

The Changing Meanings and Values of Work

Regardless of objective workplace conditions, however, societies often succeed in developing systems of meaning that rationalize and justify even the hardest labor. A saying from the Middle Ages ran: "Peeling potatoes is as important as building cathedrals, if done for the greater glory of God." It is doubtful whether many scullery maids actually took comfort in such bromides, but at least a widely shared belief system lent credibility and even honor to the dirty jobs people had to perform. Perhaps the most stikingly successful device ever created for maintaining an unequal division of labor has been the Hindu caste system, in which an advanced, complex civilization was until recently able to enforce the inheritance of jobs. If a person had the bad luck of being born to a father who was a garbage picker, then the only position open to the son was as a garbage picker in turn, or in the case of a daughter, to marry one. In some Indian states an individual of a lower caste could not even come closer than thirty feet or so to one from a higher caste; a street sweeper in Kerala had to keep at least a hundred feet away from a Brahmin at all times. What was so remarkable about this arrangement is that it survived for so long without engendering major conflicts. Its success was due to a large extent to the elaborate religious stories that explained the origins and reasons for such a division of labor, which apparently were compelling enough to keep people in their places.

Whereas the Hindu religion supported the acceptance of one's position in life, in Europe religious beliefs eventually came to justify an opposite attitude. The "Protestant work ethic" arose during the Reformation, when John Calvin's doctrine of predestination came to be interpreted to mean that a person could determine God's intentions about his or her salvation by how successful he was in this life. Thus, a man who made a good living through hard work was surely slated for heaven after he died—God would not play tricks and reward with wealth someone destined for hell. Conversely a man who could not distinguish himself in this life was probably not going to spend any time in heaven. This creed motivated Calvinists to work with redoubled energy, encouraged by the promise of an eternity of bliss. In such a framework, a job was not merely something to do for a living, but a divine "calling," a role planned by God Himself. When coupled with new technologies and forms of social organization, this ethic helped propel European nations into a trajectory of material abundance they still enjoy today.

Traces of the Calvinist ethos continue to survive in American culture, especially in the higher echelons of the economy. Many captains of industry who control enormous wealth nevertheless lead frugal lives and believe that personal good fortune must be reciprocated with charity and commitment to good causes. Among the wealthy who take on social responsibilities and philanthropy, one still finds a clear sense of calling, even though the original dogmatic rationale for them has become tenuous. Richard DeVos, CEO of Amway, reflects a common view when he says: "The most important thing to pass on is a faith in God. It impacts everything you do." And Sir John Templeton: "My ethical principle in the first place was: 'Where could I use my talents that God gave me to help the most people?' "

For the great majority, however, work as a vehicle for salvation is now an utterly alien notion. Nevertheless, adults in general still feel quite positive about their work. There are many reasons why this is so, and the specific one that applies depends on the personality of the individual worker. What is attractive about a given job to one person may well seem a disadvantage to another. For instance, by the time they are in high school American teenagers who hope to become medical doctors say more often than their peers that they want to help people and improve society. Teenagers who plan to go into business, on the other hand, state that they want to make money and have lots of free time. And so on and on: Each job has a particular profile of advantages and disadvantages that appeal to different people. Engineering is attractive to those who want to "build, create things," while accounting attracts those for whom "making money" and "having a desk job" are important. Given the variety of occupational options that are available, we are approaching the point where each person can aspire to (although not always obtain) a job that will best suit his or her temperament and preferences.

In reality, of course, the employment market is even more complicated, for not only do different jobs offer a different menu of options, but the same job may vary enormously depending on its setting. The experience of a doctor in a small-town family practice will be quite unlike that of one employed by an inner-city HMO. An accountant working for himself and one hired by a giant consulting firm will face distinct benefits, and headaches, in what is ostensibly the same job.

Given this diversity, it is no wonder that employers try to simplify matters by assuming that their employees are little more than acquiescent mechanical robots that are better managed through "command and control." The oldest motivational tools—the stick and the carrot—may be sufficient to staff a workplace in a buyers' market for labor. But knowledge workers are not inclined to think of themselves as robots, and if an organization wants to keep their loyalty, it would do best to provide an environment in which their work has meaning and value.

What does flow theory suggest are the main obstacles in our culture that prevent workers from finding meaning and value in their work? In the first place, the obvious answer has to do with the goals of work itself. *Our consumer culture has done much to devalue work* in general, by extolling the virtues of relaxation, material comfort, and pleasure—all marketable commodities for which more and more customers are needed. By age twelve children have learned that anything labeled "work" is unpleasant; conversely, if they regard something as unpleasant, they label it "work." The result is that, no matter how exciting and fulfilling a job may be, we confront it with a generalized bias against work learned early in life.

At the same time, *some jobs do in fact contribute nothing valuable or meaningful,* and thus they make it difficult for workers to get involved in them for other than monetary reasons. It is difficult to leave home for work in the morning with a spring to one's step if one's employer manufactures weapons of mass destruction, or pollutes the environment, or recklessly exploits human and natural capital. Difficult, but not impossible: Karl Adolf Eichmann, supreme dispatcher of Jews during World War II, took great pride in getting his freight trains to carry their human cargo according to schedule. One hopes that such denial, such technocratic tunnel vision, is not as common as it sometimes seems to be.

Occasionally work that appeared perfectly harmless, even noble, has turned out to have undreamed-of potential for evil. Until half a century ago physicists could be confident that their work only helped to describe the beautiful symmetry of material creation, and if it had any practical applications at all, they were bound to be beneficial to humankind. Niels Bohr, one of the greatest and most humanitarian among them, insisted until the early 1940s that the experiments with nuclear fission he was conducting in his Copenhagen laboratory could never be used as the basis for weapons. Of course after 1945 no physicist could ever again feel complacent about the possible misuses of his work. Perhaps this is one explanation for the subsequent migration of brilliant young scientists away from physics and into molecular biology, which likewise promised only benefits to humankind. But as genetic engineering comes of age, bringing with it the possibility of various forms of eugenics, even this choice appears to have its dangers.

In fact "good work"—work that is both well executed and of benefit to humanity—is not as easy to come by as one would think. A central task of management is to refrain from making it even more difficult to pursue by emphasizing greed, cutting corners in quality, ignoring the needs of workers and customers, and generally transforming the organization into a soulless, valueless enterprise. Otherwise the warnings Peter Drucker sounded years ago will come true: namely, that the brightest young people, the ones who want to have flow in their work, will turn away from business and move into nonprofit NGOs like the Red Cross, the Nature Conservancy, and academia, where the pay is less but the work is more meaningful.

Another cultural obstacle to flow is *the impermanence of post-modern business organizations.* It is difficult to devote a good portion of one's life to a cause or an entity that may disappear tomorrow, victim of a whim on the part of owners seeking a few more percentage points of profit. One prerequisite of flow is the ability to concentrate on goals without concern for anything irrelevant to the task. But how can one achieve such focus if the environment is unstable and may even come crashing down at any minute? The prudent employee will understandably divide her attention between the job, and alternative opportunities available on the market. This is not an optimal situation either for her performance or for her state of mind, but what choice does she have? The absence of loyalty on the part of workers is a perfectly logical response to the absence of loyalty on the part of employers.

Finally it should be obvious that *if management views workers not as valuable, unique individuals* but as tools to be discarded when no longer needed, then employees will also regard the firm as nothing more than a machine for issuing paychecks, with no other value or meaning. Under such conditions it is difficult to do a good job, let alone to enjoy one's work. But as Lincoln said, most people cannot be fooled for long, and few people will keep investing their psychic energy into an organization that despises them.

The Role of Attitudes

Even the best workplace conditions and the most admirable cultural values cannot guarantee that a person will find intrinsic motivation in work. As we noted earlier, young people grow up with differing amounts of social capital, whether in the form of parenting, schooling, or community resources. Some learn to develop psychological capital; others do not. By the time they enter the workforce, some are so brainwashed by the culture that they cannot see a job as anything but that, a *job.* They lack both the curiosity and perseverance that would make it possible for them to enjoy what they do. Others consider their job a *career* that will lead them to increasingly greater responsibilities and rewards. They take their work seriously, and they might enjoy it when the conditions are right. Still others regard a job as a *vocation,* so fundamentally a part of themselves that they could not think of doing anything else—like the guard in his tower at the city gates, whom Goethe describes as "born to see, destined to watch," or like so many artists, scientists, writers, and mechanics nowadays who prize their jobs beyond all measure.

I came across a good example of the latter a few years ago, when the TV show *Good Morning America* was planning a segment on flow. The producer called from New York asking if I could give her the names of some research subjects who would be good to interview about what it means to be in flow. I responded—perhaps mistakenly—that I would prefer not to do so, because it might well be seen as an invasion of privacy by the people who had participated in our research. "So what should we do?" asked the producer dejectedly. "Just take the elevator, go down to the sidewalk, and stop a few pedestrians passing by," I suggested. "In a few minutes you should have some good stories."

The producer remained doubtful, but the following morning she called with a great deal of excitement. "We have some wonderful people, some great stories" she said, and she was right. The first interview was with an elderly man whose job was to make lox sandwiches in a Manhattan deli. He spent his entire day slicing salmon—that was the extent of the challenges he encountered at work. One might have expected him to have found his task boring, but he discussed it with the enthusiasm of a poet or a surgeon.

He described how every fish he picked up was different from its predecessor. He would hold the fish by its tail and slap it against the marble counter, looking at it and feeling it ripple until he developed a three-dimensional mental X ray of its anatomy. Then he would pick up one of his five knives—which he sharpened to perfection several times a day—and go about the business of slicing the fish as finely as possible with the fewest moves, discarding the least amount of good meat. It was an excellent illustration of how by paying attention one can transform even the least promising task into a complex, satisfying activity. For that man cutting fish was not a job, but an enjoyable vocation.

It could be argued that the delicatessen worker is in a dead-end position, and that no matter how much he perfects his salmon slicing, he will be unable to grow beyond a low ceiling of complexity. While objectively speaking that is true, some people do seem perfectly happy to hone a skill to its utmost limits even though that skill is not held in high esteem by anyone else. For others, however, a job provides a lifelong opportunity to keep building psychological capital—they keep meeting new challenges, develop new skills, and grow in the process.

Monsanto's Robert Shapiro describes what he thinks is wrong with the way most managers think of their employees' work, and what he would do differently:

> The notion of job implies that there's been some supreme architect who designed this system so that a lot of parts fit together and produce whatever the desired output is. No one in a job can see the whole. When we ask you to join us, we are saying, "Do you have the skills and the willingness to shape yourself in this way so that you will fit into this big machine? Because somebody did this job before you, somebody who was different from you. Someone will do it after you. Those parts of you that aren't relevant to that job, please just forget about. Those shortcomings that you have that really don't enable you to fill this job, please at least try to fake, so that we can all have the impression that you're doing this job."
>
> It's a Procrustean concept, and it studiously and systematically avoids using the most valuable part of you, the part of you that makes you different from other people, that makes you uniquely you. If we want to be a great institution, that's where we ought to be looking. We ought to be saying, "What can *you* bring to this that's going to help?" Not, "Here's the job, just do it."

The one destructive attitude that many workers learn from badly managed jobs (and from the popular wisdom of the culture) is *to get away with as little effort as possible.* Cutting corners, passing the buck, malingering, and taking advantage of the job are often considered canny moves—a way to beat the system. But taking such a course more often than not boomerangs back on those who resort to it. In the first place, workers who expend only the minimum effort deprive themselves of the opportunity of finding flow in their work, and are particularly likely to end up bored or apathetic. Second, they reduce their chances for advancement and end up victims of a self-fulfilling prophecy, because given their attitude, nobody considers them worthy of promotion.

Motivation is rarely a factor used in judging employees, who are typically held to the standards of performance alone. Timothy Rowe describes the situation well:

> [A]t the highest levels of management in business, people are almost never interested in the reasons that a business goal isn't achieved. . . . you find over time, by experience, that there are some people who, when faced with a challenge [that is] seemingly insurmountable— the competition has one hundred percent market share, we have zero, nobody knows about us—somehow seem to be successful. They go out there; they take ten percent, twenty percent, thirty percent, forty percent market share. Through force of will, through clever ideas, they make possible something that didn't seem to be possible.
>
> Other people, when given a task which may seem relatively straightforward—you have one hundred percent market share and your competitor has zero—lose it. They're one hundred, now they're at ninety, now they're at eighty, now they're at seventy. And they can say, "Well, the reason was that our technology in product B was delayed, and their technology and the similar product came out, and so the market really recognized their technology as better. There was nothing I could have done active about it because that wasn't my prob-

lem; that was the technology department's problem." And the technology department says, "Well, we had no idea that there was an interest in this technology. You weren't on top of the fact that the competitor was going to come out with this new technology that was popular. If you told us a year earlier, we would have been happy to come out with it." You can always take any given situation and dissect it, and there's always a finger pointing in another direction. You begin to realize that it's useless to even dissect the reasons why something didn't work out. You say, "It was your product area; you were in charge; I expected you to make magic happen." And, if you maintain that one hundred percent market share, or if you took it from zero to fifty, great. But if you took it from fifty to zero, then it's your responsibility. And, that is a very real politic, hard, harsh perspective, because it doesn't admit the possibility that you did all the right things, but it just didn't work out.

From this perspective, trying to find out why an employee can't perform "magic" is acknowledged to be a waste of time. But an organization where only success counts, and one in which an employee who does all the right things and fails is evaluated by the same measure as one who fails because of ineptitude, is an organization that is not likely to generate a great deal of loyalty. It is part of management's function to recognize and reward the performance *and* the attitude of employees, and not just their success, which may be due entirely to fortuitous circumstances.

What, realistically, can managers do about the attitude of their workforce? After all, they have no control over the psychological capital of the workers they hire and cannot unmake bad habits of long standing. But they can at least affect the culture of the company through selective hiring and advancement. Nothing destroys the morale of a group as quickly as knowing that self-serving, cynical employees are promoted ahead of those who love the work for

its own sake and believe in helping the entire organization realize
its potentials.

Recent history suggests that there seem to be generational cycles among young people in terms of the degree to which they
value material benefits. In the 1950s entering college students in
the United States said that "being well-off financially" was more important or essential to them than having a "meaningful philosophy of life." By 1965 the tables had turned: Meaningful philosophy
beat financial well-being 83 percent to 44 percent. Each year afterward the pendulum has swung back toward the other direction:
By 1999, 76 percent of the entering college students said that being well-off was very important or essential, and only 40 percent
said that a meaningful life philosophy was. Christine Comaford
Lynch of Artemis Ventures reflects on this trend:

> I meet a lot of twenty-somethings who are just like,
> "Rape, pillage, make my millions, buy a Ferrari, get a
> huge house, okay, and now I'll just do it again and again
> and again and again." And that's not what it's about. It's
> about building stuff, and learning and growing and
> making a difference. So I worry a little bit. And look at
> all the day traders, and then they started getting margin
> calls and they started shooting their families.

Practically speaking, there is not much that management can
undertake to reverse such large-scale social trends. Yet each organization can take a stand by either contributing to the problem, or
trying to ameliorate it. If more business firms took seriously their
responsibility to the true bottom line, attitudes toward work would
soon change for the better. Leaders can address this issue in three
ways: by making work conditions more conducive to flow, by clari-
fying the values that give meaning to work, and by influencing the
worker's attitude in the direction that will make them both more
happy and more productive. How this can be done will be explored in more detail in the following chapters.

Chapter 6

Building Flow in Organizations

People often think that to be a successful leader in business one must above all know a great deal about what the organization does—namely, the product or service in which it specializes. While this is surely a valuable skill, the main task of a manager is to get people to work together efficiently. In their book about companies that have been successful over a long period of time, *Built to Last*, James Collins and Jerry Porras write that their leaders "concentrate primarily on building an organization ... rather than hitting a market just right with a visionary product idea and riding the growth curve of an attractive product life cycle."

An ideal organization is one in which each worker's potentialities find room for expression. As J. Irwin Miller of Cummins Engines says:

> The truth of the matter in business is that you don't do anything by yourself. You have to create an atmosphere in which people want to give their best. You don't order anybody to do their best. You couldn't order Beethoven to compose the Ninth Symphony. He's got to want to do it. And so the head of a business is an enabler rather than a doer.

As I have argued in previous chapters, getting employees to give their best does not mean exploiting their talents as a means of generating higher profits. It is first and foremost a way to make it possible for them to grow as individuals, thus contributing to the true bottom line, which is to enhance happiness.

The best strategy for creating such an organization is to provide the conditions that make it conducive for workers to experience flow. Realistically, it is not possible for anyone to influence directly whether another person will enter flow, but by shaping the environment appropriately, one can increase considerably the likelihood of its occurring.

How does such a place look? It is difficult to generalize, because each firm is so different in so many dimensions that to have them all propitious to flow is quite rare. But some companies do clearly stand out as being happy places, while others communicate a sense of dysfunction and malaise. The most obvious distinctive feature is the *physical environment.* In the famous pioneering Hawthorne experiments conducted at the Oak Park assembly works in the 1930s, industrial psychologists studied the effects of environmental variables such as lighting on worker productivity. The fact that better conditions did not prove to raise output has convinced many that the environment is not a signifcant factor. In fact, that study only measured productivity, and not well-being.

In the heroic days of a new enterprise, knowledge workers can be happy and do stupendous work in dismal surroundings, as they did at the famous Skunk Works or the Manhattan Project, or in the garages and warehouses where the pioneers of the computer revolution toiled happily around the clock. Once past its heady beginnings, however, an operation that wants to retain good workers should pay attention to its environment. It is not by chance that smart young people are drawn to such attractive locales as Silicon Valley and Salt Lake City, or to campuses such as the Redmond headquarters of Microsoft. But plush, ostentatious surroundings are not necessary, and can be even counterproductive. One of the happiest company headquarters I have ever visited is that of the outdoor equipment maker Patagonia, nestled in a set of recently refurbished factory buildings from the 1930s, in a sleepy neighborhood of Ventura, California. The entrance hallway is lined with surfboards that its employees have leaned against the wall. Yvon Chouinard describes the rationale behind this:

> I'm a businessman, but I'm still going to do it on my own terms. I'm going to break a lot of rules and we're going to blur the distinction between work and play. So we have a policy here—it's called "Let My People Go Surfing." A policy which is, when the surf comes up, anybody can just go surfing. Any time of the day, you just take off and go surfing. . . . That attitude changes your whole life. If your life is set up so that you can drop anything when the surf comes up, it changes the whole way you do your life. And it has changed this whole company here.

The Allensbach Institute, the premier public opinion polling organization in Germany, is located in a few fifteenth-century farmhouses along a lakeshore in southern Germany. A walk along its cobblestoned paths transports the visitor back to the Middle Ages, even as computers are humming softly in the half-timbered haylofts. The traveling companies of the Cirque du Soleil actually take with them the disassembled sets of a village square, which they erect wherever the circus stops, to create a familiar setting. The children of the performers go to classes in the same schoolhouse whether they are in Vienna or in Stockholm, and everyone eats at the familiar restaurants around the square.

Robert Shapiro describes how the architecture of the workplace, and the clothes workers are expected to wear on the job, can send very clear messages that support the structure of the organization:

Well, both dress and the way offices used to be designed were powerful signals of hierarchy, of power, and were designed to impress, intimidate, and frighten . . . those without power. . . . I could hear the voice of [Company Name] talking to me, and what that voice was saying was, "We are very big, and you are very small." And the obvious implication was, "Just go along, and no one will get hurt.". . . . That was what the architecture said.

In work environments that produce flow one often hears the voices of children. Building child-care facilities next to the workplace is not only a convenience for harried parents, but a return to a more natural way of living, before age segregation eroded the links between generations. Similarly, cheerful cafeterias that serve appetizing food, and places to relax, can make a vast difference in the impersonal atmosphere of the workplace. Anita Roddick explains how she evaluates the character of a company: "I always . . . look at the lavatories and look at the canteen—is it a bloody dull place?" Unfortunately, the majority of them are.

This sentiment is shared by William Pollard, who relates how the physical arrangement of the offices is a concrete manifestation of the firm's philosophy:

[T]he question you just asked is constantly being asked within the company, and being asked of people within the company. "How is this being translated into how we run this business? How we treat our customers? What products we have? What services we deliver? How we design, for example, this office?" If you walk through the office, one of the principles you'd see is nobody works behind closed doors. Everything is open. That doesn't just come because somebody said, "It's nice to have everything open." It's come because there's a fundamental belief in how you think people ought to work together. . . . it's part of having a philosophy of life.

Douglas Yearley of Phelps Dodge offers an example of how changing the physical environment can be the first step in changing the entire culture of an organization:

> When I was running the Los Angeles plant I was still a "little kid" in my thirties, and the principles that I applied there I still apply today. I remember, when I started up the factory, I went in early, at six o'clock in the morning, the first day I took over. . . . When I turned the machines on there were rats running all over the place. So I said, "We obviously have a housekeeping problem. Let me see the safety record." Terrible safety record, big workman's compensation charges, quality problems. People were not proud of what they were doing. And so I started spending four hours a day on the floor and I'd walk around to the various machines and I'd talk to the operators and I'd say, "What can we do better here? We've got a problem, this is something that we have to do together or else we're not going to make it." We started with housekeeping and safety. The place got painted, sparkling, people felt good about it. The roof had panes in it that hadn't been cleaned in thirty years and suddenly we had California sunshine coming through. The place was bright again, you could see if you had a defect. And [we had] contests. I'd go around with my white gloves and declare a department the cleanest that day and they'd get donuts or pizza or something. . . . In two years it made money, it was a great success.

Environmental conditions that impact on flow don't necessarily have to be in the workplace itself. For instance the daily commute can have significant effects on the productivity and well-being of workers. The problem of getting to work is not a new one: Sicilian farmers had to rise at three or four in the morning to saddle their donkeys for the long trek to their distant fields. But at

least their ride was probably more serene than the two hours
spent in stop-and-go traffic that so many workers have to endure
before they stagger out of their cars, exhausted and stressed, in
the company parking lot. Forward-looking companies are beginning to provide busing to their far-flung employees who have no
access to public transportation, a measure that not only saves fuel
and aggravation, but allows riders to catch up on reading, and
helps form relationships between employees who work in different departments and would not normally meet.

Of course, as with all good things, there is a point of diminishing returns after which trying to provide for workers' comforts
begins to resemble interference. After World War II the typewriter
(and later computer) giant Olivetti embarked on a utopian experiment and rebuilt its facilities near Ivrea in northern Italy as a
rolling campus with modern buildings of outstanding design. They
included athletic fields and swimming pools, as well as concert
halls and theaters where professional casts performed. But at the
time, the resortlike establishment was felt by the staff to be patron-
izing, and the unions suspected it was a management ploy to co-
opt the workers. Union leaders even now often take the attitude
that management should limit itself to issuing the paychecks, and
leave the well-being of the workers to their elected respresentatives.

In addition to the physical environment, another clue to the
quality of life at a workplace is the *demeanor of its people*. Where
there is little opportunity for flow workers tend to be sullen, and
look defeated and worn out. By contrast in an environment conducive to flow their movements are light and exuberant, and the
halls are filled with joking and smiling. On a large scale, one
could until recently see this difference simply by driving from
West to East Germany. Passing the border checkpoint with its
barbed wire and police dogs was like stepping into a world whose
citizens were chronically angry and suspicious. It is remarkable
how easily conditions can be created that make life seem either
bitter or full of promise.

There are many steps management can take to make the emotional environment of a company lively and welcoming. Some of these are largely self-evident. For instance, in an ongoing study of outstanding colleges, we are interviewing faculty, students, trustees, and alumni to discover what makes these schools so exceptional. At one liberal arts institution the majority of the respondents mentioned the president of the school, and among his virtues the one most often cited was his sense of humor. He never took himself too seriously, he lightened up meetings with funny remarks, and he participated in student parties. Any such signal from management that while work must be taken seriously, it is not all there is to life, is bound to have a liberating effect on the morale of the organization.

More substantive ways of improving the business environment involve setting policies that allow people to move and act with freedom, to have control over their tasks, and to have input in decisions affecting their work. In the rest of this chapter we shall review in greater detail how these strategies can help build an organization in which work can become a flow experience.

The Prerequisite for Flow

It's impossible to create an environment that will foster flow without commitment from top management. Leadership must embrace the idea that before products, profit, and market share they are primarily responsible for the emotional well-being of their workers. Few CEOs approach this task with the exuberance of Anita Roddick, who relates how she occasionally starts a board meeting or a conference with financial investors by announcing: "Well, I think we are not going to grow next year. We just want to have more fun." (And, she adds: "You can see them blanching.")

Not everyone would feel comfortable working—or investing—in a business that puts fun before financial growth. There will always be companies that take themselves very seriously, that play the market game as if it reflected ultimate reality. Many employees continue to prefer to dress in pinstripes, clutch their briefcases for security, and follow unquestioningly the rules they were given. But if we are concerned with growth and happiness, not business as usual, then we ought to consider how to transform the dreary confines of ordinary jobs into places that stimulate flow.

Many leaders are already implementing the main conditions that make flow possible, or at least they understand how to do so in theory. For instance, Mike Murray of Microsoft describes the three "common things" that determine the success of a business team:

> [Number one:] If the manager makes sure that every team member has very clear goals that line up to what the company needs to be doing . . . Number two: if the manager is really good at planning all the incremental activities that need to get done so that the work flows smoothly through the team. And number three, if the manager is really good at keeping communication and feedback . . .

Note how in a few concise sentences Murray defines the factors— clear goals, good feedback, incremental challenges—that stimulate the growth of the worker's skills and allow flow to occur as well as contribute to the effectiveness of the team. Of course, as the old saying goes, there is an ocean between saying and doing. So how *does* one implement these valuable ideas?

Clarifying Organizational Goals

It is difficult for workers to focus on achieving company goals if those goals are not understood—or worse, if they are misunderstood. Perhaps the most often mentioned trait of a healthy organization is communication based on trust. Unless subordinates can trust their leader's commitment to the firm's vision and values, and unless the leader can trust his subordinates to be candid, the organization will soon self-destruct. A good example of how trust works in a company is one given by Max DePree, the CEO of the office furniture manufacturing company Herman Miller, whose sales manager was about to conclude a multimillion-dollar deal with a military base. At that point the base supply officer let it be known that he expected a payoff for awarding the contract, even though it was the lowest bid. Phil, the sales manager, informed the customer that his company would not do such a thing.

"Sure," the supply officer replied, "everybody does it."

"No," Phil said. "We don't."

"Well, I'm going to have to call your boss, and you'll probably lose your job."

And Phil answered, "Oh, no, we just lose the order."

The reason Phil could act with such assurance was that he was confident that the CEO would back up his decision not to make a payoff even if it meant forfeiting the order. He trusted his boss, who in turn could trust Phil to abide by the values of the company. The story ended well, according to DePree:

> And we got the order, because the guy couldn't go back to his superior and explain why he wasn't able to give the low bidder the order. But in a case like that, Phil had to know me quite well in order to just put that on the line, and say, "Well, we can lose the order. We can live with that." I think one of the jobs of leaders is to make that very clear to people in the organization.

A very similar story was related by William Stavnopoulos, CEO of Dow Chemical, who defines the shared values of the company as its "culture":

> To give you just one example: About two years ago, I guess it was, we were in very delicate negotiations with another company. I was not personally involved. People

who worked for me were doing it. And we were getting close to a negotiated settlement. The other company recommended an outcome that was I guess, legally, probably correct. But it didn't smell right, you know? It just didn't feel right to our people. They left the meeting. And it was financially very advantageous to us—very advantageous! They left the meeting, refused to take it, and then called me and told me about it—they refused. That's a natural instinct. They all felt that way at that meeting. It wasn't that they had to call me and ask what I think. They just automatically reacted that way.

That's having a culture . . . a strong culture. Then you have to be proud of the people that do that. And that's what we try to strive for here. These are natural reflexes. You don't have to think about that. You don't have to think about those things. You just don't do it.

There are several reason why such goals are not clear in many organizations, and it is useful to review them to see if they apply to your own company. In the first place, it could be the case that *the mission of the organization* (or team or individual worker) *is unclear to everyone,* including the top leadership. In other words, not even the CEO or the board has confronted the task of defining the purpose of the organization. If this indeed is the case, it is the responsibility of the next level of management to raise this issue with the superior and try to resolve it. Every well-run organization has not only a good business plan, but a set of core values that are expressed in the behavior of the leadership and are continuously reinforced through written statements and verbal communication.

Most business leaders would agree with Anita Roddick about the importance of communication: "I think that is one of the most essential skills of leadership. Because no matter how passionate you feel about something, if you can't communicate it in an enlivening or entertaining way, and if you can't have a passion, which is the most persuasive form in communication, you might as well just not be there. I've watched so many people with such good intent, and they flounder. They just have no knowledge. It's an art. It is a *definite* art, a skill."

Gillette's former CEO, Alfred Zeien's philosophy of business leadership is that one should spend 90 percent of one's time on the "three Ps": People, product, purpose. While selecting, training, and promoting staff is the most time-consuming element, providing purpose is equally essential: "People say, what do you mean by 'purpose?' Purpose is the time that you spend with people constantly going over and over and over in their minds, what is the purpose of this whole undertaking. Why are you doing that job? Why are we on this particular crusade? What's the purpose of this enterprise? What's the purpose of your contribution? There's a little bit of preaching involved in that. Some people say it's motivation. I say, it's more than motivation. It's creating a sense of purpose in an organization. Whether I was a supervisor of just fifteen people or forty-five thousand people, it [didn't] change all that much."

Second, *the mission is unclear to the line managers.* Many people in positions of authority are afraid to seem uninformed, and prefer to fly blind rather than admit their ignorance. Yet the saying that the only bad question is the one that isn't asked holds especially true in this context. There are many ways to clarify the goals of one's team or division, including spending time in solitude and reflection, and by talking with one's peers, subordinates, and superiors. Usually a combination of these strategies works best: Thinking things out for oneself is essential, but so is reality checking with informed colleagues.

Third, it could be *that the mission is unclear to one's subordinates.* This is probably the most frequent cause of confusion in an organization, and it could be due to several factors. We too often take it for granted that just because we understand a situation, it is clear to others as well. Making certain that everyone is on the same page seems like a waste of time, so we tend to do it less and less often—despite the fact that new recruits are constantly entering the system and fundamental conditions are changing. Frontline workers may soon develop a distorted view of the company's priorities, not to mention what is expected of them. Richard DeVos of Amway describes one strategy for guaranteeing that company goals are well understood throughout the organization:

> I make sure [the staff is] informed. All the years we ran the company, for example, we had an employee meeting every month. [We did so] out of respect for employees, [and because we wanted] them to be a part of the company. Once a month, we have a meeting—it takes about an hour—and inform them of how business was, whether it was up or down, what the conditions were. We'd answer their questions about why we did or didn't do certain things, why we had this benefit and not that benefit. We would discuss with them why they all didn't have a parking place at the front door. Since there were several thousand cars, somebody was going to have to park in the back end. It sort of depended on who got there on time. Anyway, things like that we have fun with at our meetings.
>
> So, that's showing respect for people. When you communicate with people, you show your respect for them.

Even under the best of conditions information decays rapidly as it is disseminated in groups. The psychologist Donald Campbell ran a series of experiments years ago that were modeled on the popular children's game "post office." He had college students sit in a line of chairs, and read to the first of them in private a story that the student was then to tell the next student, and so on, until it reached the last one, who was then asked to write it down on a piece of paper. As you might expect, the story that reached the end of the group bore little resemblance to the one at the start. If the initial account was about John poisoning his wife Mary, it was not unusual to end with Mary's poisoning John.

Such confusion is common in every organization, and the only way to combat it is to make systematic efforts to keep lines of communication open. The most effective means of doing so is to set aside time to have occasional conversations with each team member, during which they can be questioned about what they think the main goals of their work are. In lieu of this informal approach, the same purpose can be achieved in public meetings.

It is also useful for the manager to reflect on whether it is he that unconsciously keeps his workers in the dark. It is not unusual for managers who are insecure in their position to use "divide and conquer" tactics, keeping vital information to themselves, or releasing it unequally to their staff. This might be a useful tactic in the short run, but sooner or later it will lead to confusion and demoralize the team.

While the long-term goals of an organization will typically be quite stable, its day-to-day priorities are likely to change, sometimes so gradually that they are not noticed. Unless management is diligent in redefining the goals, and keeping everyone notified of any changes in direction or policy, sheer momentum will continue to keep the group on its accustomed path for some time to come. Whenever change becomes significant, it helps to have a meeting that combines an appreciation of past accomplishments with an explanation of the new priorities and the reasons for adopting them.

Christine Comaford Lynch offers one of her usual colorful takes on why communication is so important, especially in small start-ups that employ knowledge workers in a rapidly changing environment:

> When you grow really fast, the people at the bottom of the food chain don't know what's going on. How can they get emotionally engaged? They feel out of the loop, and when the suits are all talking, they don't know

what they're talking about. So I think communication is huge, and I see some start-ups do a really good job, every Friday have beer, and the CEO does a short, not boring [presentation]. "Here's where we're marching— we all want to name the next product, let's all generate ideas and whoever wins gets five thousand bucks" or whatever. It's a community, we're speaking of communities. Setting it up so that people can thrive, and not just survive.

Performance Goals

Merely having organizational purposes clearly defined is not a sufficient condition to experience flow, for one must also know, moment by moment, what precisely needs to be done and how well. There are jobs in which every step of the activity is spelled out in advance—as is typically the case in assembly-line work—but most leave quite a bit more leeway as to how they should be performed. For instance, it is clear that a salesman's aim is to conclude a sale as quickly and profitably as possible. However, each sale requires a somewhat different approach: Should he be pushy or laid back, jocose or serious, authoritative or friendly? And what aspect of the product should he emphasize—price, convenience, reliability, appropriateness for intended use? The answers to these questions depend on many variables that cannot be predicted in advance, such as the customer's mood, needs, and even the time of day and the weather. A good salesman intuitively selects a particular strategy appropriate to the occasion, and follows the chosen script at least until it proves to be the wrong one.

In many organizations, especially large bureaucratic ones, a great deal of time and energy are wasted in meetings and procedures that are meaningless to the participants, and leave them exhausted. Deborah Besemer of BrassRing Systems makes it a rule to clarify the immediate goal of each staff meeting: "When I start a meeting with anybody in the company we start off with, 'Okay, what's the purpose of this meeting? We are in danger of wasting five people's time for one hour, that's five hours of company time, let's establish why we're here.' "

People are frequently unable to define their own goals and rules of operation—they can conscientiously follow what they are told to do, but are wary of improvising or changing strategies when they reach an impasse. In many endeavors such lack of initiative can only lead to disaster. Mountaineers prepare their routes obsessively, and it is not unusual for a climbing team to spend days at the base of an intended climb, checking the rock face through telescopes, and planning each of the hundreds of moves they will make after they start. Such advance work will usually ensure a successful climb. Quite often, however, once the team is on its way the route will look quite different than it did from base camp. The rock could be looser than expected, more covered with ice, more overhanging. Unless the team is willing to shift to an alternative route, should the circumstances demand it, they might pay for it dearly. The same ability to stay focused on one's intended goal but to change strategies when necessary is what ensures success in any other activity, from chess to surgery to business.

What can a manager do to foster flexibility in performance goals? Like anything else, the best course is to allow people to learn by doing, and if necessary, by failing. It makes sense to start by assigning a person a task without very specific instructions for how to achieve it. For example, ask a subordinate to write a request to the general manager explaining why the team should be allocated a larger budget next year. Then with the report in hand, ask its author to explain the purpose of each paragraph, perhaps even each line and word contained in it. Why were these specific words used to describe the situation? Why did he stress these particular issues? Why did he present them in that order?

The point of such an exercise is to demonstrate that every step in writing a report reflects a choice, that every word—like each move of a climber on a rock—should be carefully aimed to reach the intended goal. At the same time, it should be stressed that there is not one "right" way to draft such a document. The form it eventually takes depends on factors like the personal interests of the GM, the current priorities of the firm, the recent performance of the team—perhaps even the weather and time of day. Whether one's subordinates market bubble gum or design landing gear for jumbo jets, it is important to let them *experience* that everything they do is under their control, that every procedure is beneficial to the extent that it helps the group as a whole reach its objectives.

Occasionally one encounters individuals who are so good at finding flow in their work that they will take a job with very restrictive parameters and turn it into something much more interesting by adapting performance goals to their own needs, even though no one else but them is aware of it. For instance, there are busy homemakers who actually look forward to ironing, because even though their spouse and children may not notice the difference, they themselves set such high standards for how well an ironed shirt should look that they can feel a sense of accomplishment similar to that of an artist examining a just-completed canvas. There are assembly-line workers who set for themselves the goal of halving the time it takes to reach their quota, even when it has no particular advantage for them, because the pace of the line cannot be exceeded. They are not rewarded with a bonus or recognition, but they do enjoy the same satisfaction as an athlete who keeps besting his personal records.

What underlies this ability to set goals is a willingness to pay attention to what one does, to invest psychic energy in one's actions and their results. Unfortunately many workers come to their jobs without the psychological capital that would enable them to develop effective strategies independently. They are too afraid of failing, or too bored to be bothered. They will do what they are told, but cannot conceive of a better way of doing things. The only recourse then is for the manager to put the employees who show no initiative in situations where they have to learn to sink or swim—with the manager serving as a helpful but determined lifeguard.

How Well Am I Doing?

Knowing precisely what task needs to be done is useful only inso-far as one also knows step by step whether the goal is getting closer. Imagine wanting to get to a flashlight placed at the other end of a large, dark hall. You want desperately to reach it, but suppose that you are also blindfolded and your hands are tied up so that you can't use them for exploring in the dark. No matter how deter-mined you might be, you would still be soon frustrated at having no idea whether you were making progress or simply going in circles.

While not as bad as this imaginary scenario, poorly designed jobs often cause people to flounder for lack of information about their performance. To keep apprised of one's progress and firmly focused on the task at hand, three major sources of feedback are worth developing as a routine part of one's activities. The first is *feedback from other people.* This falls under the more general topic of "communication" discussed earlier, which many managers feel is the most important aspect of their responsibilities, and which is often lacking in their organizations.

Top executives take steps to guarantee that they themselves receive feedback by being constantly in touch with their peers in related businesses, and internally with key personnel in their own firm. For instance, when John Reed led Citicorp, he met at least twice a year personally with the half dozen heads of the major world banks, and even more often than that with the CEOs of companies like GM, GE, or IBM. He also spent at least half the morning talking on the phone with the thirty or so people of his inner network at Citicorp, and never made a major decision with-out consulting at least some of them.

In a less formal way, Anita Roddick is also always absorbing in-formation: "I'm a great talker. I'm on the bloody phone talking whenever I'm in, anywhere I can pick up the phone to seven or eight people I adore around the world . . . and we just rap and talk." Timothy Rowe uses the phone in a similar way:

> I do something we call a "kitchen cabinet," which is a voice conference call that I do with a friend in Madrid, a friend in San Francisco, and a friend who has been in London until recently, and myself. We get on the phone every couple of weeks and just talk for a couple of hours about what's going on. . . . These are long-time personal friends, and we use each other as kind of a sounding board for the things that we're doing in our lives, by providing some disinterested insight.

Many executives build up a support system of peers and experts in other organizations, to whom they can turn to in times of need. Apple Computer cofounder Mike Markkula says: "For thirty years there have been people I could call and say, here is my problem. They were always supportive." Of course such networks do not arise automatically; one must be trusting, open, and willing to reciprocate, qualities that are not always valued in a business environment.

To successfully manage an organization one should also know its parts intimately—especially the people who make it function. Enrico Randone, former CEO of Assicurazioni Generali, one of the largest European insurance companies, claimed that as he moved up in the organization he got to know personally almost ten thousand branch managers dispersed from Milan to Manila, and that it was this familiarity with the staff that eventually resulted in his claiming the top job.

J. Irwin Miller of Cummins uses an example from antiquity to stress how essential it is for a leader to become closely acquainted with and listen to the people in the organization:

> The very best leaders have always been enablers. That goes even back to classical times. I don't know if it was in

Thucydides or not, but there was a Greek general . . .
who was beloved by his soldiers because he behaved exactly as present-day business consultants are advising
CEOs to behave. . . . He knew all his people. He talked
to them. He asked their advice. He seriously considered
it. And he reported back to them. He sounded like the
way Peter Drucker is advising today, and that was 2,500
years ago.

In a large organization it is frequently difficult for a leader to
have an accurate sense of the company's affairs because reports
are often afraid to be candid about problems. The head of a large
multinational corporation employs the following strategy to keep
the lines of communication and feedback open:

Two weeks ago, I spent one entire week—five days—
traveling to seven different cities and having meetings
with employees. I talked to two to three hundred employees twice a day—different employees—for maybe
an hour, giving them my views and then leaving an hour
and half for them to ask me any questions they had.
That's how you keep your finger on the pulse.
    . . . I've got to get out and be with customers and be
with employees and be in the field and watch what goes
on and provide motivation. Last week I was in Asia all
week. The same thing. I was visiting our staff, visiting
our plants, showing an interest in what they're doing.
That's how you do it. You don't do it sitting here.

Deborah Besemer describes another important source of
feedback:

I think there are a lot of ways that you can check your
progress. One is you can check with your clients. You
can check your reputation in the marketplace and I

think your values shape what your reputation is. We survey our clients; they had never done that here before.
We are now twice a year surveying our clients as to what
they think of us.

All too often managers are hesitant to allow others to influence
their own decisions, resulting in the "Fire, aim, ready" sequence
typical of so many wasteful efforts. Or they hide behind the "not
enough time" mantra, even though strategic consultations held
before a major decision is implemented would save a great amount
of time in the long run.

It is equally important that managers provide the kind of feedback that will enable members of the team to enjoy work and grow
in the process. Like every other aspect of the job, this requires investing a portion of one's reserves of psychic energy. One must
pay attention to the details of each subordinate's performance,
note his strengths and weaknesses. Yearly evaluations are not suffi-
cent; even quarterly or monthly feedback is often too general to
be of much help. A good manager is like a conductor on the
podium during a concert, straining to hear how each of the in-
struments in the orchestra is playing, now toning down the brass
section, now asking for more sound from the winds, while leading
the entire ensemble in harmony.

There are many ways to pay attention to performance, some as
institutionalized as the practice Richard DeVos describes:

Which led us to having a PR department go through
and find in the press stories of people who are doing
unusual things and good things. And there are a lot of
those people in the world that most of the time aren't
written up in the paper. And so we began a little program of writing them a letter of congratulations, which I
would sign. Ten or fifteen years later, they would say,
'Oh, you wrote me a letter.' Cheerleading isn't big stuff,
it's just a lot of little stuff every day.

Of course because paying attention to "a lot of little stuff every day" can take up a great deal of a manager's time, feedback can also be provided by mentors. Almost every business leader remembers individuals who have helped him to improve his performance during his career. Most of these mentors were more experienced colleagues whose temperament and values were congenial, rather than people who were appointed to the role. Deborah Besemer points out one reason mentors are important:

> Because you have to be able to say things to your mentor that you can't say to your boss. Or shouldn't say to your boss. Like "My boss is a jerk. How do I work on this situation?" Or some of the things you might need mentoring on are your relationships with your colleagues. "I don't know how to work with this guy. He's driving me nuts. I think he's a slimeball." Or whatever. I wouldn't go to my boss and say that.

Immediate, specific feedback is one of the most effective tools to help workers improve their performance. Depending on the business you are in, this may involve walking the shop floor every day, or reading memos, or checking plans, or tracking sales figures—and in the process always asking questions, soliciting opinions, commenting, suggesting, praising, and correcting. Of course, the danger of overdoing this kind of feedback is "micromanagement"; one likewise has to learn to restrain from interfering when things are going well. Micromanagement gets its deservedly bad reputation from the fact that those who indulge in it usually believe that they alone know the right way of doing things, and they want everyone else to follow their example. A manager will prove herself to be far wiser when she tries to learn, with the help of the worker, how the job could be done better.

A well-established finding in social psychology is that it is less effective to tell a person, "You did this wrong," than to say, "Let's see if it could be done better another way." When you focus a comment on another individual (*You* did this . . .) all sorts of defenses spring up in his mind, interfering with his ability and motivation to learn. Whereas if the comment is directed at the performance itself, it is interpreted as being less threatening, and consequently the likelihood of learning increases.

The second source of information is *feedback from the work itself.* Some jobs have built-in measures of performance: so many widgets turned out during the day with X number of defects or so many units sold to customers. In most occupations, however, results are not so obvious. The success of some recent management techniques, like TQM, are in part due to the fact that they help organizations to quantify the performance of the firm. Unfortunately, the methods of doing so are sometimes quite arbitrary and fail to reflect real value. But having benchmarks to gauge one's efforts is seductive, and makes the job more enjoyable for those who use them.

Whatever technique is employed, it is the manager's responsibility to spell out expectations clearly, so that workers have access to them and can evaluate how well they are doing in meeting them. At the same time, managers should set up comparable signposts for their own performance. Some CEOs have "to-do" lists, and even lists of lists, that they update every day. Every item one checks off upon completion provides a little jolt of satisfaction.

Finally, *feedback can come from one's personal standards.* A real leader depends less on external signals than on an internal sense of what constitutes a well-done job. Such conviction is based on experience, but often it becomes so much a part of oneself that it seems an intuitive, natural judgment.

It is not easy for managers to instill this sense in their workers. The best strategy is to establish one's own standards clearly, and then take every opportunity to apply them at work so that others can come to recognize and learn from them. In some cases this may involve redoing a job several times, even under time pressure, until it's as close to perfection as possible. Alternatively if the leader cuts corners, everyone else will conclude that standards are not to be taken seriously and can be abandoned whenever it is convenient.

If performance is growing lax, it pays to make a public case out of a project as an occasion to reaffirm basic standards. Without placing blame on or embarrassing those involved, one should review the circumstances and evaluate each step of the process with the management committee, asking suggestions about ways to improve it.

Obtaining and providing feedback are time-consuming, and can use up most of a leader's psychic energy. Yet such activity is time well spent, for without it there is no way of knowing the true status of an organization, which in turn makes leadership impossible. The stream of information that flows through an organization is its lifeblood, allowing adaptive responses to internal and external changes. And more to the point, in the absence of feedback there is no learning, and there is no growth—only routine, mechanized apathy.

Matching Challenges with Skills

The work environment will determine to a large extent how fully a person employed in it can develop. Some people will find ways to do their best no matter where they are placed, but it is the manager's responsibility to provide the opportunities for each worker's skills to be used and refined to their fullest. "Skills" in this sense does not refer only to technique and knowledge, in the sense of "engineering skills," for example, but to the entire range of human capacities a person possesses, including values, emotions, humor, and compassion. Unless all of these can be expressed on the job, the workplace will not be one in which complexity can flourish.

The first and most obvious decision a manager should make when hiring is to ask: Does the candidate fit the goals and values of our organization? Companies are as diverse as New Guinea tribes are from one another. Some are fierce headhunters, others are peaceful farmers. An ambitious young woman who would feel comfortable at McKinsey might well grow bored working for L.L.Bean. A young man with strong environmental values would be an asset to Patagonia, but probably not to Exxon. Given the diversity in corporate cultures a salesperson or system designer who would be a godsend to company A, may be a failure in company B.

One cannot build a coherent organization if the people who comprise it have different values, so it is to everyone's benefit to make certain that the match is suitable. This does not mean that everyone in the company should have the same profile on the Myers-Briggs, however, for diversity of temperaments and perspectives is a very useful component in a well-balanced business. But unless basic priorities about what issues are important and how operations should proceed are shared, chaos is likely to ensue. Unfortunately we have no foolproof method of ensuring an essential fit in values, so much of the decision regarding hiring will depend on a manager's intuition.

A company can easily be destroyed if the board hires a CEO because of his success in another firm, without considering whether the outsider's values mesh with its own. The core values of any organization tend to be eroded by every new hire who—rightly or not—holds contrary ones. This is the reason why the "visionary companies" studied by Collins and Porras almost exclusively promoted their leaders from inside, while the companies that folded tended to seek "saviors" from outside the firm.

Once a person is hired, it makes sense to start him at the least demanding level, where the challenges are lowest. In that position a supervisor can assess easily the newcomer's strengths and weaknesses, while permitting him to make mistakes that will not have dire consequences. Alternatively, some firms prefer to throw the recent hires in at the deep end of the pool, so to speak, and see if they survive. While this is a procedure that may save time, by winnowing out unsuitable staff, it also results in a great deal of turnover and premature burnout.

One can easily judge what a person is made of by assigning him such simple tasks as addressing envelopes or filing, or comparable work for staff at higher positions. Napoleon used to say that you can't become a good general if you haven't learned to take orders from a sergeant. An employee's personal weaknesses often reveal themselves in the way he cuts corners or sloughs off a simple job. This provides an ideal opportunity for a manager to begin giving the appropriate feedback, and to start the employee on the right footing.

At the same time one must be alert to when the employee is ready to assume the next stage of responsibility. Burnout is caused not only by too much work, but also by too little. It is not easy to navigate between stress and boredom, but a manager must assume that challenge and set workers on a course that will allow them to fulfill their potential.

In assessing the suitable level of challenge for employees, it helps to know their particular skills. A number of psychological tests have been designed to measure cognitive capacities, or categorize native traits—such as extroversion, perseverance, or creativity. Not so long ago, people were advised to study the results of these tests and then work on those areas where they were weakest, such as vocabulary or negotiating skills. Current opinion favors the opposite approach: Determine your strengths, and build upon them. It is certainly more enjoyable, as well as more productive, to work from one's proficiencies instead of struggling against the grain—provided one has the opportunity to apply that expertise in the organization.

It may be useful at this point to return to Figure 2 in Chapter 4. Referring to the diagram, how much time do you think your most valuable staff members spend in the various "channels" of the figure? Does one often look stressed, and another depressed? Could this have anything to do with the challenges of the tasks they have been assigned, and if so, what could you do to bring them into the focused flow zone? As a matter of fact, it wouldn't be a bad idea also to ask these questions of yourself.

The ideal balance between challenges and skills never remains stable for long. Either one or the other component predominates, at which point adjustments will be necessary. An employee who is getting married, or buying a house, or having a baby will come to work with some of his psychic energy already committed to dealing with the changes in his personal life, so he may be stressed by work challenges that earlier he could take in stride. In such cases a good manager may want to ease up on his workload until the situation stabilizes.

Deborah Besemer describes one way of dealing with such situations:

> One of the things we do is to find out from conversations with the employee, is this a temporary situation or is this sort of a basic thing? Because sometimes [there's] a temporary situation where they're having to deal with somebody they don't want to deal with, whether it's an unhappy customer or a colleague or whatever. Is that short term or is that a long-term, endemic kind of thing, [in which] there isn't a match between what makes you happy at work and what we need done. And that would be a cause to split off. Or is it a temporary situation, and then what can we do to make it better?
>
> . . . Balance is one of the issues that goes up and down a lot. You're unhappy in your job because you don't have time for anything else—it has become all encompassing. And I watch that really hard because one of the things I've seen over the years is the number of people that burn out. And what can we do about that? Is this a temporary situation that because we're about to get a product out that you're working nights and weekends and crazy hours, or is it a culture that we have set at this company that we expect everybody to work those hours, or is it that your skill set really isn't up to the job so that you're having to work that many hours to get the job done?

There may come a time when an employee's performance is so unsatisfactory that the only solution is letting him go. Managers generally find having to fire a subordinate the worst part of their job. Mike Markkula is someone who developed a method to improve on the match of skills and challenges as an alternative to firing. He calls it the "Peter Recycle Principle," a variation on the notorious "Peter Principle":

> I would go to that person and say, "You're not cutting it, but your skills look like you might be better suited for this other job over here. It happens not to pay as much, but if you get on this track and you are successful, then maybe you could go back up again. But we can't keep doing what we are doing." And some people would get their ego stomped on and quit. Others would go do [the other job], and several of those people really excelled. So that was one way of dealing with it.

The important factor to keep in mind is that personal growth is contingent on the balance of opportunities for action and the capacities to act that a person encounters at work. Some of the most significant chances to achieve differentiation and integration are those presented by the job. It is difficult to become a complex person if work does not encourage the development of one's unique skills, nor the sense of being part of a common enterprise.

The constant availability of new challenges is one of the elements of business that makes it so exhilarating. It is this feature that most business leaders cite when they are asked what they like most about their job. James Davis is inspired by "the challenge, and building the team—but that's all part of the challenge, too. I mean it's the challenge more than anything else." Deborah Besemer explains:

> I love the pace. I love the way things change and change quickly, and that you're always confronted with new

challenges because of that pace of change. I get very excited by challenge and growth. I hate downsizing. Hate
it. I've done that. I really don't like it. I like building
teams of people. I get really motivated by it. I . . . I'm almost a parent in the pride I have in the employees.

The theme of growth spurred by new challenges is echoed by
many leaders, including Jack Greenberg of McDonald's:

I think if you don't grow, you shrink. It's not like you
can keep the status quo. I don't think it's possible in
business. So our founder used to say: "If you're green,
you're growing; and if you're ripe, you rot.". . . You need
growth to stimulate people to keep an interest in the
business, to keep them energized and to build an organization that provides opportunities that can support
community effort and that makes profit.

Another condition that makes work more flowlike is *the opportunity to concentrate.* In many jobs, constant interruptions build up
to a state of chronic emergency and distraction. Stress is not so
much the product of hard work, as it is of having to switch attention from one task to the other without having any control over
the process. If a person who is working on a problem for hours is
interrupted by a phone call, it may take another half hour afterward to get her mind back to the point where it was before the
call. When person A comes by to discuss his problems, you have to
reorganize your mind to see things from his point of view, which is
fine. But when B, C, and D stop in one after the other with their issues, and each requires that you clear your mind of the previous
set and refurnish it with the elements of new personalities, and
their specific problems, that can take a toll on consciousness quite
quickly. After a few hours, your brain feels like a quivering mass of
jelly.

The manager who does not set some time aside for reflection every day is likely to be headed for a burnout. And the manager who does not actively protect his subordinates' psychic energy from being disrupted is going to have a frustrated staff. It takes trust to respect a closed door, or private space in the maze of cubbyholes; but the manager who encourages workers to set a "Do Not Disturb" policy when necessary is not likely to regret it.

Concentration can be disrupted not only by colleagues, but by such things as the products of new technologies. One of the most interesting recent cases is the Internet. E-mail is a wonderful invention that expedites communication beyond one's wildest dreams. When in 1583 the Jesuit priest Matteo Ricci established his mission in China, it took more than a year for a letter from him to reach the order's home office in Europe, and he had to wait another year to receive a reply. Now in a matter of minutes you can get the answer to a question from Beijing. At the same time, it is easy to form a dependence on this steady flow of information. There are managers so preoccupied with their e-mail messages that they never look up from their screens to see what's happening in the nondigital world. Each query requires an immediate answer, and they feel guilty for the least delay. As with other wonders of technology one must draw a line and reassert control over the medium. The world is not going to fall apart if you refuse to be enslaved by your inbox. If all else fails, the company should consider offering workshops on how to manage an e-mail stream without interfering with the rest of the job.

Much has been written about how *control over one's job* contributes to work satisfaction, so little more needs to be said here about this topic in relation to flow. It should be noted, however, that what the term "control" implies is often misunderstood. Some people believe they are in control only if all the parameters of a situation are exactly as they want them to be. The "control freak" demands that everyone do things precisely as he wishes, and he follows rules obsessively—everything must be "just so." A controlling person does not respect the independence of his colleagues, and this sort of control is not the kind one experiences in flow.

A surgeon cannot be in full control of the operation, because there are simply too many unforeseen eventualities that may occur—the patient's organism may react unexpectedly to the anaesthetic, or to the trauma. The poet is not in complete control of the poem she writes, because each new word suggests unexpected ideas and feelings that demand responses. What "control" means in these cases, rather, is the feeling that if the occasion requires it, the individuals involved have the necessary skills to set new strategies to reach the ultimate goal—to cure the patient, to write a good poem.

This is precisely the latitude of control that should be available on the job for employees to be in flow. They should be able to feel that they have a choice over how to perform their job, that they are trusted to come up with the best approach that a given situation requires. However, in this case, too, technology can be easily misused. For instance, a large utility company decides to give its service workers cell phones and location devices that can pinpoint their whereabouts within the distance of a city block. A central computer monitors incoming service calls, and depending on the problem involved, contacts the closest worker and instructs him to proceed to the caller's destination with the tools and supplies needed to fix the problem. For each worker, the computer also calculates the quickest travel route.

There is no question that this procedure is wonderfully efficient, rational, and sensible. But as a result of it service workers who previously had only a specific area to cover are now being sent to emergencies in new districts. Before the system's introduction they had to plan their own route, and establish priorities independently. By being deprived of these choices, the worker suddenly feels like a cog in a machine rather than a free agent troubleshooter.

Whenever a new technology is introduced, it pays to ask the

question: How will this affect enjoyment of the work? It would not be difficult to adapt the computerized location device so that it could come primarily under control of the person in the field rather than the central office. The choices he makes can still be monitored, and if wasteful they can be addressed by his manager. In the meantime, however, it is likely that the worker in the field will have more flow without such restrictive control—and probably be more productive in the long run, as well.

Christine Comaford Lynch, a venture capitalist in Silicon Valley, defines the issues involved in controlling workers quite clearly:

> I see a lot of "control freakism." So I love when people empower others, because you just get loyalty, you just get somebody totally motivated. And probably someone who is going to give you a lot of creative cycles, like in the shower they'll be thinking, "How can I really optimize that marketing campaign?" Because it's their baby. That makes such a difference, so I love when I see that. And you do see that at some big companies, but I just find the start-up world is much more fun, 'cause risk is rewarded, instead of punished. So that empowering thing is huge, and supporting people and giving them a chance.

One aspect of control deserves special mention, and that is *control of time*. We have seen that a person immersed in flow loses the strict sense of clock time. Rhythms of effort and relaxation follow each other organically, in response to the activity itself and the person's internal states, not to an abstract system of measuring time. In the last two centuries, however, human activity has increasingly been shaped by schedules set by the needs of industrial production. When Stalin decided to modernize the USSR, he ordered that workers who showed up at the factory late more than twice a week should be shot. Needless to say, it took a while for Russian farmers unfamiliar with industrial time to get used to punctuality.

Few aspects of work have changed so much in the last decades as the rigidity of scheduling; the trend has become increasingly a return to a more flexible allocation of time. It is estimated that currently up to 40 percent of knowledge workers in the fastest-growing occupations in the United States work nonstandard hours. At many companies, such as the Gallup Organization in Nebraska, employees negotiate the time a task is expected to be accomplished, and then they are free to do it at night or the weekends while staying at home during the week.

Finally, the last condition that is universally mentioned as part of the flow experience is the *loss of ego*. Our concern for the self is so strong that if anything makes us self-conscious, it attracts our attention at the expense of our complete involvement with the task. Any instance of personal criticism will do so, but so will inappropriate praise. Our immediate response is to begin thinking about being fired or being promoted; either is a distraction that interrupts flow, not only at the moment, but sometimes for the rest of the day, and beyond.

Therefore it is critical to remember what was said above in the section on feedback: One should focus on the performance, not the person. Some managers like to flaunt their power by dressing down workers in front of their colleagues. This is an urge that would be better to resist, because nothing creates havoc in consciousness more damagingly than public humiliation. If one must be critical of a subordinate, it should take place in a one-on-one encounter.

An employee who is always self-conscious, watching the effect he has on others, who is vain and jealous of others' success, who insists on standing on his rights and keeps score of perks, has probably not accrued enough psychological capital to be able to enter flow easily, and to remain in it. He can be helped by counseling, and by being given trust and responsibility so that, if he can manage to overcome his insecurities, he can become fully involved in his tasks. It helps, of course, if the manager can keep his own ego at bay. Again, modeling behavior is the appropriate way to set the tone in an organization. If the boss always has to take credit for every accomplishment, if success is more important to him than the quality of work, it soon becomes clear to everyone what the true priorities are.

Many leaders confronting succession issues base their choice of who will assume their title on whether the candidate is ego-driven or has the best interests of the organization foremost on her agenda. Giving a promotion to someone who puts her own interest ahead of the group's goals gives the wrong signal to the rest of the staff: It says that to get ahead in the company one must be selfish. Leaders who care for the welfare of their organizations share J. Irwin Miller's concerns:

> Too many of the young people that we get out of business school, their major aim is to say, "I want to make a million dollars before I'm thirty." They don't say: "I want to do a good job, or help to build a company." There's nothing much selfless in them, and they are doomed to failure if there isn't a selfless quality in their own values.

Miller's comment is also true in the context of flow. Excessive selfishness leads to failure because one becomes insensitive to the joys of doing a good job, of helping others, of helping to build a company. From the perspective of the true bottom line, people with such agendas can never be regarded as successful.

Part III

Flow and the Self

Chapter 7

The Soul of Business

Merely providing all the necessary ingredients for flow is not sufficient to guarantee that an organization will be a gratifying place to work. Just as climbers need a mountain peak to get their juices going, or a surgeon needs a health emergency to get involved, workers need a compelling reason to focus their energies on the job. C. William Pollard writes: "People want to work for a cause, not just for a living." A paycheck is a sufficient impetus to motivate some employees to do the minimum amount to get by, and for others, the challenge of getting ahead in the organization provides a satisfactory focus for a while. But these incentives alone are rarely strong enough to inspire workers to give their best to their work. For this a vision is needed, an overarching goal that gives meaning to the job, so that an individual can forget himself in the task and experience flow without doubts or regrets. The most important component of such a vision is an ingredient we may call soul.

What Is Soul?

"Soul" is a rather old-fashioned word. It has been abandoned by philosophers ever since Kant declared that attempting to define it was a hopeless task, and more than a hundred years ago William James deleted it from the psychological lexicon by arguing that it was superfluous for scientific purposes. Today the concept of soul keeps a precarious foothold only in the realm of religion. Yet the idea that there is a vital essence that cannot be reduced to the matter from which the body is constructed still has a strong hold on our thinking. How can we explain it in terms of current scientific understanding? And what relevance, if any, does it have to the management of business?

What we call soul is a manifestation of the complexity achieved by our nervous system. Every organization of matter, after its components reach a certain threshold of complexity, will exhibit traits that did not exist at lower levels of organization. Atomic forces, electromagnetic forces, and the force of gravity impose order on matter at different levels of inorganic structure. When inorganic molecules finally combined with one another to synthesize light and to reproduce, they became plants, which were "alive" in a way that minerals were not. For this reason, philosophers attributed to them a "vegetative soul," which was thought to be something added on to their inert material substance. Now, however, we would say that whatever makes plants alive is not a vital element added to inorganic matter, but the outcome of inorganic matter itself having reached a certain complexity, which resulted in life.

Similarly, past explanations attributed to animals a "sensitive soul" to explain the fact that they could move around and experience sensations in ways plants could not. In this case again we would explain the difference not in terms of a unique vital substance that separates plants from animals, but as the behavior appropriate to organisms that have developed a more differentiated and integrated level of material organization. Finally, because human beings show evidence of thinking, willing, and perceiving, they were deemed to have a "rational soul" that enabled them to do such things. In many religions, the human soul was also believed to partake of the divine essence implanted by God into our bodies.

Again, one can explain the phenomena that made our ancestors believe in a soul by assuming that when our nervous system achieved a degree of complexity that no other living tissue had previously achieved, the processes of thinking, feeling, and willing were made possible. Humans thus developed *self-reflective consciousness,* or the ability to examine what went on in the mind, as it were, from the outside, and as if it were a new form of objective reality— even though the phenomena thus observed took place only within the neurons and synapses of the brain.

But this still does not account for all that we intuitively mean by "soul." After all, when we speak of a "soulless banker" we don't usually mean that the banker in question literally cannot think, will, or feel. Or when we say that a cocker spaniel has a "soulful look," we don't necessarily imply that it can think, will, or feel more deeply than the banker. There is more to soul than even these wonderful achievements of consciousness.

Perhaps the best way to explain what the word "soul" connotes is that, no matter how complex a system is, we judge it as having no soul if all its energies are devoted merely to keeping itself alive and growing. We attribute soul to those entities that use some portion of their energy not only for their own sake, but to make contact with other beings and care for them. In this framework, the soulless banker has no attention left for anything but his own goals, while we believe the cocker spaniel is loyal and selfless. (Of course, we may simply have been seduced by its big brown eyes— but that's besides the point.)

Thus we infer the existence of soul when a system uses some of its surplus energy to reach outside itself and invest it in another system, becoming in the process a stakeholder in an entity larger than itself. At the human level curiosity, empathy, generosity, responsibility, and charity are some of its noteworthy manifestations. The most familiar example of soul in action is when a person devotes attention not just to selfish interests, or even to material goals in general, but to the needs of others, or to the cosmic forces that we assume must rule the universe. The religious meaning of "soul" therefore derives from the efforts that some individuals undertake to worship the divinity.

The ability to transcend self-interest is presumably a recent capacity of human consciousness, which is itself the result of the human nervous system's having reached a complex level of material organization. But this explanation should not be taken as reductive: It does not imply that soul is nothing but matter. On the contrary, the fact that a material organism has somehow become able to reach out to other beings, and to see itself part of a cosmic pattern, is an extraordinary step in evolution. Obviously, we are not always, or even very often soul-full beings. The centripetal forces of selfishness are still too strong within our nature. Given all the threats from the environment and from people who are not our kin, we could not survive for long if we didn't devote most of our attention to self-preservation. But if we expended all our energies solely on taking care of our own needs we would stop growing. In that respect what we call "soul" can be viewed as the surplus energy that can be invested into change and transformation. As such, it is the cutting edge of evolution.

There was once a word that described a person who acted in accordance with these principles, but it is seldom used now. The term "magnanimous" referred to someone with a large soul (from the Latin *magnus* = great and *animus* = soul). Both a warrior who forgave his defeated enemies and a rich man who distributed alms to the poor were considered to be magnanimous. (In Hindi the comparable term *mahatma,* which also means "great soul," was the title given to respected spiritual leaders, including Mohandas Gandhi.) But perhaps it was because this honorific was usually bestowed on powerful individuals that it fell into disuse; it offends our democratic sensibilities to have the actions of those who can afford to be generous given a special moral value.

Rather than throwing out the concept of magnanimity because it has been misused, however, we may want to revive it and apply it more generally to anyone who behaves in a disinterested way, no matter how humble or wealthy he is. A retired nurse who volunteers at a free clinic is just as magnanimous, relative to her social capital, as Andrew Carnegie, who donated millions of dollars to build public libraries.

Having briefly examined the concept of soul, let us now turn to how it relates to organizations, and to business in particular.

Soul and Vision

When people in business discuss "vision," they are usually referring to the articulation of soul. In other words, vision is the expression of a way of being that does not exist yet; it is the anticipation of a future state of the organization. Vision requires the investment of energy (that is, financial, social, and psychological capital) in order to transform the present system into a new, desirable form. Thus, vision can be defined as the anticipated evolution of an organization that has become conscious of its own potentialities.

Among the business leaders we have interviewed, most endorse a vision for their companies that is characterized by soulfulness: namely, it extends beyond the interests of the owners and shareholders, and reaches out to wider goals. One of the most frequently mentioned objectives of this sort is *the attempt to achieve excellence.* Being the best at what one does certainly brings financial profits and renown, and so this quest may in large part involve selfish goals. But there is also a transcendent, evolutionary motivation for being the best—reaching for a Platonic ideal of perfection that draws one to a higher level of performance, and perhaps of material organization as well.

For instance, when Norman Augustine of Lockheed Martin was asked what was the most important thing he wanted to accomplish in his job, he answered:

> Probably the legalistic answer would be that what I was trying to accomplish was to increase shareholder value. But in truth, what I was trying to build was the greatest aerospace company in the world. And I thought that if

we did that, maybe that would increase shareholder value.
But to me, you have to have a more lofty goal than making money.

By our definition, this quote is an expression of soul. It focuses
attention away from the present, from the self and its interests,
toward a more desirable future state that does not yet exist. Another name we give to such a vision is *creativity*—the process by
which new objects and new ways of doing things come into being.
Jack Greenberg of McDonald's also wants his organization to be
the best in the business:

We have the vision of being the world's best quick-
service restaurant experience. We are already the
biggest. . . . To us, the best means to be the best in every
country, in every market, in every restaurant for every
customer every time.

But striving for excellence does not necessarily demand that
one become the best in one's field. For many, it means simply to
do one's personal best, or the best that the organization can accomplish given the financial and human capital upon which it can
draw. Ultimately what makes a result excellent is that it goes beyond what one would have expected given the available resources.

The second manner in which soul is manifested in the vision of
leaders is by *doing something of benefit to others.* Sir John Templeton
expressed this value in its pithiest form: "Those who give, get;
those who try to get, don't." Or as Ted Turner said:

If you want to have a sense of real accomplishment, you
are going to do a lot better if you don't just make money
selling junk to people. That you create something of
lasting value, of benefit to humankind and to the
environment.

Quite often the people to whom one is attempting to reach out are the employees of the organization itself. In this case the vision of the company involves creating an intimate, humane environment in which to work. Though the following observation may sound sexist, it is remarkable how often it has been women executives who placed a special emphasis on this goal. For instance Anita Roddick explains: "I love the relationship I have with my franchises. With my employees, who are my most treasured, loved friends. They are my extended family." Christine Comaford Lynch, an impresario of venture capital, extends her love of people to her clients:

> I just love connecting people. Because it's like chemistry class. I put this and this together and see what happens! Sometimes it explodes, but usually it works out. [laughs] Something better is created. I really like bringing people together.

What Comaford Lynch is creating with her psychic energy is a new set of relationships, a new social organism, as it were. And this organism would not exist if she had invested her attention exclusively in her own selfish goals.

Most of the leaders we interviewed are involved in philanthropic projects ranging from the establishment of summer camps for ghetto children to building concert halls, endowing schools, and other civic initiatives. It is not only money they give, but the rarer contribution of their time and attention. In either case they typically consider these activities as a natural extension of the values of the organization. Richard Jacobsen of WSJ Properties expresses a sentiment that most have shared in one form or another: "I felt like it would be challenging, interesting and satisfying for us to try to take some of our talent and expertise that we had gained in the business world, and see if we could put it to work in the community." When the challenges of the business organization are under control, a whole new set of opportunities opens up in the larger world.

A few leaders are in the process of combining business and philanthropy in original ways. For instance, 10 percent of Patagonia profits go to support environmental causes. Each year the workers elect from the pool of employees a committee that decides how these funds should be allocated. Yvon Chouinard explains his vision: "Our mission statement is to use business to find solutions to a lot of this environmental crisis. And I'm constantly pushing everyone in the company to realize that's why we are in business. That is the reason. We are not in the business to make a profit. We're not in the business to make a product. We're in the business to really change the way other companies operate."

Some follow their altruistic vision to the point that they feel they can no longer fulfill their responsibilities to the organization because larger commitments demand too much of their energies. For instance Don Williams, as CEO of Trammell Crow, the commercial real-estate company, had been involving his organization in philanthropic activities for years. Eventually there came a time when he felt he should step down to continue working for the common good:

> For me, today, work is a platform for social involvement. . . . My passion today is focused on the comprehensive renewal of our lowest income neighborhoods in Dallas. . . . It is unjust in America for so many of our people to not receive a good education, not to have access to a decent job, and not to have access to a decent home. That is an injustice. By the way, if you don't have an educated workforce coming up, if we have a society that is eroded overwhelmingly with drugs and crime, that's not good for business. Now that's not the model under which I do that, but I think there's a case there that's very good for business to take home.

Quite often the vision involves values based on *a religious faith.* This is not surprising; after all, in the past religions have been the prime repositories of the dreams for a better world. The major world religions have all insisted that there is more to existence than the material body, and they have taught that excessive selfishness is evil. By directing attention away from biologically programmed instincts and drives they have shown the way for the evolving soul. Even in a high-tech company such as Microsoft there are leaders like Michael Murray whose vision is based on religious faith:

> I sin, I make errors, I'm imperfect, but I'm committed to trying to correct those so that I can become what God would want me to be on this earth, and achieve all the potential that is within me. . . . I feel a life obligation to Him to do that.

Richard DeVos makes the point that even if religious values are not always explicitly observed, they still help a person to make decisions in a consistent and effective way:

> Now, as you and I know, none of us lives up to that fully. But, nevertheless, that becomes your goal and your guide, and when you go astray, you know where you went astray. If you don't have that, you have nothing to go against because you don't have anything to stand up for. Then anything goes, anything's accepted when there are no values. I don't know what people do who don't have a value system. Then, what is right or wrong? You don't know. Anything you decide is right, is right.

The values derived from religion are almost universally regarded as complementing sound business practices, rather than contradicting them. What J. Irwin Miller of Cummins Engines says would be confirmed by most respondents:

I grew up in a family that believed in the values of the Christian religion, in a broad rather than a denominational aspect. And I believe that responsible behavior can also be described as good long-range planning. I don't see anything difficult about ethical behavior. I see a lot of difficulties in making short-cuts and trying to make end-runs around responsible behavior, and usually you regret it exceedingly. In the long run ethical behavior . . . is just the sensible way for business to operate.

A somewhat similar point is made by Jack Greenberg of McDonald's:

Giving back to the community that you're in business in, is good business. It's the right thing to do, because you have a social obligation, it seems to me—businesses as well as individuals. But it's also good for business. It surely helped build our brand. We don't do it for that reason. The motive is different. But the result is the same.

Having the opportunity to draw upon the cultural capital of a religion—the accumulated wisdom of many generations—can also save a great deal of psychic energy. The person who follows religious prescriptions does not have to question each decision she makes—right and wrong appear clear. Instead of ruminating on what *should* be done, one can actually *do* things. The meaning of life is not in doubt, which helps the believer avoid depression and the terror of death. The downside, of course, is that over time religions become encrusted with precepts and ideas that are the antithesis of soul, as each faith tries to protect its doctrines and institution instead of nurturing the evolution of consciousness. If one is not careful to distinguish the genuine insights of a religion from its irrelevant accretions, one can go through life following an inappropriate moral compass.

Christine Comaford Lynch, who has adopted a Buddhist phi-

losophy of life after spending years in meditation and apprentic-
ing as a monk in a monastery, describes how these experiences
guide her in using her surplus energy to help others:

> But I think that when people ask you for help . . . you
> should just jump in and help. Because, there is nothing
> in it for you initially, but it sets in motion this energy
> that I can not describe. When I was younger, I used to
> think, "I did such and such for Suzie-Q, so when I call
> her she should deliver." And then I realized how stupid
> that was, and that it doesn't work that way. When you
> help people out, other people, not necessarily the same
> people, will help you out. It just gets something rolling.
> Like when you are fortunate financially and you give
> money away. More money comes your way. There's
> some sort of "laws of the universe" that I think I'm start-
> ing to figure out. So a big part of it is helping people. I
> really think it makes a difference.

In contrast, Sir John Templeton gives a definition of egotism
that vividly describes a vision that is short on soul:

> Well I'm not very clear on it, but, I think of egotism as
> looking towards yourself, and I think of love as looking
> outward. And so, our job, in order to serve God, or be
> more Godlike, is to focus on how much good you can
> do to others, and give very little thought to whether it's
> going to rebound to you. You can't keep it from re-
> bounding to you.

If one chooses not to rely on a religious tradition, one must
nevertheless find for oneself a system of meanings that justifies
existence. But these meanings cannot come only from within, for
they would cease to exist at the end of our lives. Often they come
from one's relationships, as in these words from Jane Fonda:

> Like most people I want my life to have meaning. I am
> not afraid of dying, but I am afraid of getting to the end
> of my life and having lots of regrets. And regrets to me
> would be not having people left behind me who loved
> me. Children and family. That, and having a lot of things
> that I wish I had done that I didn't do. Having a life that
> really had no relevance or meaning beyond just some-
> one was born, lived, and died . . . I want to feel that my
> life had some kind of meaning.

In many ways, the search for a life that has "relevance or meaning" beyond one's material existence is the primary concern of
soul. This is precisely the need that a person who is aware of his or
her own finitude feels, the need that motivates us to become part
of something greater and more permanent. If a leader can make a
convincing case that working for the organization will provide relevance, that it will take the workers out of the shell of their mortal
frame and connect them with something more meaningful, then
his vision will generate power, and people will naturally be attracted to become part of such a company.

When a leader's vision embraces one of these goals—to do the
best possible job, to help humankind and the environment, to
obey a cosmic purpose—then the organization itself becomes invested with a soul. It does not exist solely for its own benefit, or for
the benefit of those who by investing in it have made its existence
possible. It has a purpose beyond itself and reaches out to help
other systems, to create other forms of organizations.

Still, being motivated by a transcendent vision of this kind does
not guarantee that a leader or an organization will actually act in a
soul-full way. All too often these values never progress beyond pious intentions that are used to deflect attention from selfish behavior. As discussed earlier, the more desirable something is, the
more it will be exploited by people who will mimic its form without honoring its substance. This explains why images of youth,
health, sex, and fun are so widely used to sell merchandise to

which they have no logical connection, and why patriotism, religion, and altruism are so often donned as the sheep's clothing in which ravenous wolves hide.

If, however, a vision is genuine and is carried into action, it becomes a powerful attractor for the energies of the members of an organization. It provides a goal that is worth pursuing above and beyond the extrinsic rewards that can be provided by the job. Without a vision of this kind, the only reason to work is for pay and promotion. These are strong incentives, but limited in their power to motivate. If one grows dissatisfied with one's paycheck or the chances of promotion, then the amount of psychic energy one is willing to invest in the company decreases. Whereas if the work contributes to some greater cause, the satisfaction of being part of a creative enterprise becomes a strong source of motivation that justifies the further investment of energy, even when other rewards are not as attractive.

The Stuff of Great Souls

How do certain individuals come to be so concerned with excellence, with helping people, and with following God's will, that they are able to merge their own personal goals with purposes beyond the self? At this point, we really have no good answer to that question. Most respondents in our interviews pointed to their family background as having provided them with strong values, and often with a religious faith. But it also seems clear that, for whatever reason—a quirk of genetic inheritance, or early learning—those leaders whose vision leaps out into the future started to shape their own lives from very early on. They had a curiosity, a zest for life that impelled them to seek greater and greater challenges, and to find flow in productive activities.

A large number of them came from families who were surviving just above the subsistence line, and several did not have outstanding educational backgrounds—some did not even finish high school. Their parents are often remembered as distant, not very involved with their children, but leaving them ample freedom. Despite—or because—of such early conditions, these leaders grew up with a fierce desire to succeed, coupled with a lack of self-centeredness.

In reviewing what these visionary business leaders have said and how they actually operate, five traits appear to be the most important in their attitude toward life. The first is an unbounded *optimism,* which consists in thinking well of human beings in general, and being positive about the future. Often this optimism is based on a sense of calling, or vocation—the conviction that one has a meaningful role to play on the stage of life. The second is a strong belief in the importance of *integrity,* an unwavering adherence to principles on which mutual trust can be based. A third characteristic of these individuals is a very high level of *ambition* coupled with *perseverance,* which allows them to weather hardships and to take on increasingly difficult challenges. The fourth outstanding trait is a constant *curiosity* and desire to learn. Finally, all of them mention the significance of *empathy* for others and a sense of mutual respect. It will be useful to look at each of these characteristics in greater detail.

Perhaps the most obvious trait one notices in these leaders is what one of them characterized as "pathological *optimism.*" For instance, here is how Christine Comaford Lynch answers the question as to what enabled her to be successful at what she is doing:

> Drive . . . heart. I really have this thing about contributing. I really want to contribute. I'm really driven by the high five. I should explain that because it might sound hokey, but I really believe in it. The high five to me is when I die, God-Buddha-Allah-whoever, whatever is out there, says, "Rock on, sister!" And gives me a high five. "You rocked this incarnation, you did a great job, yay!" Because I think that life really is a gift. And I think that it's really special to have the opportunity to have a lifetime, and also to just be in this time.

Not all of them would use such colorful language, but they did share the sense that life is a gift that brings with it opportunities and responsibilities. All of them are grateful to be alive in this time, which they feel is a good time, and getting better. In this respect, they express the optimism that psychologists have found to be a characteristic common to successful political leaders who can lift personal interests toward more inclusive goals.

For leaders in business, optimism is almost a necessary trait: It gives them the self-assurance needed to solve difficult problems. C. William Pollard claims that his most useful strategy when confronted with the challenges of the job is simply to believe that all problems have solutions:

> While I often don't state that, mentally that's the way I come. There has got to be a solution. There is a way to solve this. There is an answer here. There's no problem that's insolvable or too big to solve. So it comes with a mind-set of solvability. And that's probably the most important [strategy].

Byron Lewis, Sr., founder of UniWorld, a large advertising company that specializes in ethnic markets, explains how his optimism is rooted in his African American heritage:

> Black culture is founded on the belief—a religious foundation—that good things will come. In my generation, they have. I mean, I admire my forefathers because they persevered when there didn't seem to be much opportunity. . . . But we have . . . an obligation to work hard, because that's what this country, with all its faults, offers to people. And what you see in the communities of color is an absolute commitment to hard work. The newly arrived Caribbeans, the black people that came up from the South, the people who are coming from Asia, have an absolute commitment to hard work. . . .

[as well as to] strengthening the family and small business development, and I certainly should underscore
the religious foundations of many of these people. I think
religion is also a very strong element in going forward.
We see many people coming back to that.

Their optimistic appreciation of life may be the reason these
leaders can so easily find flow in their work, forgetting themselves
in the pursuit of new challenges. From the world-weary viewpoint
of many academicians this attitude may appear childishly naive.
Yet it seems to work, enabling the person who has it not only to
enjoy life, but also to work for the well-being of others. It is unfor-
tunate that we don't know how to bring more of it into our lives.

Optimism extends to a generally positive attitude toward others. Trust is such a central requirement for doing business that
unless one believes in the fundamental decency of humanity it
would be difficult to operate without becoming paranoid. Here is
how DeVos expresses this attitude:

There's a wonderful sense of duty and responsibility on
the part of most people. Otherwise, the whole system
fails. You can't do it by having a policeman at the door or
having a truant officer check up on every employee to
make sure they really are sick. You work on a basis of
trust. That's how the world runs. And, when you don't
have that trust, then the world comes apart. But our
world's running pretty well. And that's the world I live in.

Often this optimism is accompanied by a sense of calling, a
feeling that one's life has a purpose, that one is destined to accomplish great deeds. A good example is Sir John Templeton's
reminiscence from his childhood:

When I was very small, maybe as young as eight years
old, I wondered why humans were created. Why are

there humans instead of no humans? And coming from a religious town, I thought God must have made people for some purpose, and that possibly one of the purposes was to accelerate God's creativity. It's so obvious that there's great creativity going on, and that creativity is actually speeding up . . . that early lifetime viewpoint was that I wanted to make my life useful. I wanted to find out what God wanted me to do. And one of the things he might want me to do is to help speed up his creative process.

Richard Jacobsen is another leader who expresses a very similar sentiment:

It's a faith that there's some overall purpose or plan to life and that you and I occupy some place in that plan. My faith gives me that context so everything I see, I see in that context . . . to the extent that you feel like what you are doing is part of a larger picture. It's not just you doing your own thing, but you're a part of something that's bigger than you are. And I feel like I'm on the Lord's errand, and He has an interest in what I'm doing.

The same trust in a calling is voiced by Christine Comaford Lynch, who explains why her mission of empowerment is so important to her: "Just because I think it's what I'm supposed to do. That's just what I get when I say, 'Okay, God, what am I supposed to do with this incarnation? Tell me what my charter is, so I can really serve you.' "

The origins of this sense of being chosen to accomplish a significant task are not clear. In most cases there is no indication that parents or other adults thought very highly of these leaders when they were children. If anything, their modal childhood seems to have been characterized by benign neglect. Nor did they experience any dramatic life-changing events that set them on the path to their vocation. Instead, for whatever reason, these individuals seem to have started out in life with the certainty of a mission, and gradually they grew into their vocation. Their consciousness of having been called upon to do their best has not faded through the inevitable false starts, failures, and disillusions of life.

In addition to optimism, the most salient value these leaders share is a belief in *integrity,* which is a mirror image of the sense of trust discussed above. In order to trust others, one must trust oneself, and be trusted by others. All of them claim that integrity is such a basic value in their organizations that it's not even raised as an issue. As Alfred Zeien says: "I never worked in an organization on a career basis where the values were anything but integrity and transparency. I think I always said that whatever position you take, picture yourself on the witness stand before a prosecuting attorney. Would you still say the same thing?" In the opinion of these leaders it is possible to succeed in the short run by cheating and dissembling, but such dishonesty is inevitably found out, and having lost the respect of peers, those who profit from it will be shunned. As Jack Greenberg explains:

> We've got hundreds and hundreds of suppliers around the world. In many cases, we're their only client or we're ninety percent of their businesses. And all that is done on trust, by the way. We buy twelve to fourteen billion dollars worth of food and paper packaging every year on a handshake—no contracts. It's all based on the relationship and trust.

Generally their reverence for integrity seems to have developed naturally, absorbed from the atmosphere of the family. One subject mentions that he learned early on the rule that he should not do anything he would not like his mother to read about in the papers. Others describe how their fathers were respected by their coworkers, and they assumed that this was obviously the way one should behave. Robert Shapiro expands the notion of integrity into what he calls authenticity, which many others also mention in different terms—the ability to be oneself, and at the same time to be intimately concerned with others. Shapiro's notion of authenticity consists of the two dimensions of differentiation and integration, which we have earlier learned are the components of complexity, the direction in which evolution tends:

> Authenticity is about the ability to connect deeply with yourself and to be able to express yourself in coherent, integrated action. By "integrated" I mean in a way that is consistent in all dimensions. And by "caring" I mean that one's motivation needs to be something beyond either greed or fear, both of which turn out to be related phenomena. Or maybe the same phenomenon. Ideally there needs to be some sense of connection, at a minimum with the people who are engaged in the work, ideally with the people who will be affected by the work.

Two other traits that help to preserve the sense of one's vocation as an attainable ideal are strong doses of *ambition* and *perseverance*. The ambition is often expressed in a selfless form, as a desire to make one's company the best in the business, or to provide the highest-quality product. At the same time, none of the leaders denies that a good deal of personal ambition is also involved. John Sobrato is typical:

> Well, I guess the desire to be recognized as good at what you do has always been there with me. I mean, when I was in college and selling houses, it was real important to be the best salesman in the office. And same thing after I graduated. [It was] most important to be the best salesman in the real estate board. You know—all those things turned out, but I had to really work at it. . . . You're really out there driving. . . . It was a real driver for me to be the best at everything I could do.

As we know from flow theory, it is difficult to continue to enjoy the same activity unless the challenges involved in it keep increasing. Ambition is a strong motivator in keeping people enjoying what they do, as Mike Hackworth of Cirrus Logic describes: "I believe in setting very ambitious objectives. I think that you only achieve what you set out to achieve, and somebody once used an expression that stayed with me for a long time, 'a man's reach should exceed his grasp.' You should be reaching for more than you can just easily get a hold of, so I tend to set very aggressive goals, very aggressive objectives."

Perseverance is another quality all these leaders prize. Several of them proudly expressed the belief that they were probably the most determined, stubborn people we were likely to have interviewed in our study. As James Davis of New Balance says: "Tenacity, I think that's important. Integrity is important. Loyalty, it's important. Well, work ethic, that goes with tenacity, I think. It's fairly basic principles. There's nothing really complicated about it. You just make up your mind that this is what you want to do, you go do it." In many of the interviews, respondents mentioned that a key consideration for a young person who is contemplating a business career is never to give up when confronted with obstacles.

Sometimes the desire to win, to be the best, becomes such a dominant motive that the person's life becomes an endlessly enriching competition: "To me life has always been a battle or a game that I wanted to win," says Ted Turner, "like Monopoly or chess." Once life is transformed into a game with clear rules and goals it is easy to be perseverant in it because the task is so enjoyable. What to an outsider may seem grim determination driving these leaders to ceaseless work is in reality the deep involvement of flow. Jane Fonda describes it well:

> This work is in my life and in my head and my heart all the time. All the time. I'm always reading or writing or speaking or thinking or planning, but I'm sometimes doing that while I'm fishing in Montana, or hiking or

horseback riding. I'm kind of compulsive. Ted calls me a workaholic. And I don't even relate to that, because for me it's not work, it's my life. . . . That's what I do, that's what I love. It's what defines me.

But an energizing vision cannot be based only on calling and ambition. With those ingredients alone, it could remain the basis for a selfish venture that led in no new directions. The calling of visionary leaders includes a sense of incompleteness, of wanting to go beyond the boundaries of what is known. Their favorite mode of being is becoming, which reveals itself in a wide-ranging *curiosity,* an openness to all kinds of experiences. Orit Gadiesh of Bain & Co. is typical:

I read history, I read biographies, I read military history— I find them interesting. I read books about math and science—I read philosophy. Whenever I travel to a country, especially if I am on vacation, I will buy books that are written by authors in that country—it gives you a lot of insight into the way people really feel. I love theater, I love to travel. And I am curious about anything up to a point. . . . I can't become an expert on everything.

Such broad-based interest is another trait that prevents one's energies from becoming too self-centered, and allows more complex connections to be formed. All of these leaders are lifelong learners—their curiosity keeps them wanting to know more, to improve themselves. As Anita Roddick explains: "Success . . . is consistently learning how to do things better." Or Gadiesh again: "One of the things that is fun for me is to keep learning all the time." Through learning we grow, becoming more than we were before, and in that sense learning is unselfish, because it results in the transformation of what we were before, a setting aside of the old self in favor of a more complex one.

The other trait that leads one away from selfishness is *empathy,* or a sensitivity to other people's needs. We have seen over and over again how critical it is for these leaders to believe that their actions are helping their employees, their customers, society at large, and the environment in which they live. Mike Hackworth describes how empathy has benefited him:

> I think that one of the things that has helped me tremendously in my career is that I could put myself in the other guy's shoes. So whether it's in a negotiation, or in motivating people on a team to get a job done, to accomplish an extraordinary task in a short period of time . . . my being sensitive to their issues and helping them get through their issues, was due, I believe, to my empathetic nature, and that then dramatically increased their commitment to want to achieve the goals. They redoubled their energy and put more into it, and you could accomplish uncommon results.

Another leader contemplated the basis for his success: "Empathy was very key because I could sit down with the customers and understand their needs. So I think empathy had a lot to do with that." A key manifestation of empathy is *respect*. Treating peers, customers, and subordinates with respect is one of the most often repeated values endorsed by this group. As James Davis describes it: "Respect is very important. Mutual respect is very, very important. You really have to think in terms of how the other person you're working with is thinking and try to put yourself in their position." Without respect, the subtle alchemy that binds an organization or that serves as the impetus for a business transaction would dissolve into mutual suspicion and hostility.

It is interesting to compare the traits that are so salient for these exemplary businesspeople with those that are held in high esteem by leading figures in other fields, such as science or the arts. Many of the characteristics are common to both groups: Both scientists and artists also value integrity, have high ambition and perseverance, and are filled with curiosity. What sets visionary business leaders apart, however, is their unbounded optimism and trust in fellow humans, and their veneration for empathy and respect. These are found much less often among leaders in other professions, and appear to be the distinguishing features of this group.

Even if one discounts some of these claims as being to a certain extent self-serving, it is clear that what makes it possible for such leaders to be so focused in their work and so effective in advocating their vision is their genuine conviction that their efforts are helping to create a better world. It is because their message appeals to the soul, to the need we all have to connect with a greater purpose, that others are willing to follow their lead and find flow in their work.

Chapter 8

Creating Flow in Life

T o bring as much flow into one's life as possible, the first step one must take is to define one's priorities—the things one believes are worth living for. Knowledge of these will provide the ultimate goal that transforms a desultory existence into a purposeful, enjoyable adventure. It will also help shape the vision that will motivate others to invest their energies in the organization one heads. A leader will find it difficult to articulate a coherent vision unless it expresses his core values, his basic identity. Yet while everyone assumes that his or her identity is transparent, there are, in fact few things so covered with veils of deception as one's own nature. For that reason one must first embark on the formidable journey of self-discovery in order to create a vision with authentic soul.

Who Are You?

Among the most ancient words of advice that have come down in the history of our culture are the ones carved above the entrance to the Delphic oracle: "Know thyself." Philosophers ever since have repeated this injunction as the prerequisite for a happy life, and it is also one subscribed to by visionary business leaders. When asked what advice she would give a young person who is thinking of a business career, Christine Comaford Lynch replied:

I would really, really stress that they get on the path of getting to know themselves. If you're just so out there and you have no idea of who you are and what you believe in, you're going to be lost your whole lifetime. You're going to marry the wrong person, you're going to make a lot of mistakes. . . . It's going to be a problem and you're going to wake up one day whether you're twenty or fifty or ninety and go 'Uh-oh. This is really not working.' Why not learn that sooner than later? So people don't develop a relationship with themselves, and they don't develop a relationship with whatever spiritual thing they believe in. The world can be really confusing. Without that sort of foundation, how are you going to have a hope of doing the right thing? You aren't going to know what the right thing is because you haven't built any sort of foundation . . . and without that—nothing else really matters.

But how does one get to know oneself? In their responses to this question, the paths of the philosophers and the business leaders diverge. For thinkers the answer leads them through introspection, through critical reflection and a constant testing and questioning of the basis of belief and knowledge. In our times, this effort may involve the psychoanalytic project of learning the reasons for one's actions and the roots of one's neuroses. Or it could lead to the adoption of the endless critique of the deconstructionist, suspicious of all certainties. For the professional thinker, the quest for understanding is a lifetime effort that is an end in itself—a dangerous quest that can lead to nihilism, or even worse in the pilgrim's eyes, to self-deception.

This is not the way business leaders seem to approach the journey to self-knowledge. For them knowing oneself is not an end, but a means. Their ultimate goal is to act effectively in the world, and in order to do so they must learn who they are. So instead of an endless search for the root of their being they look for a core belief that can sustain them through life, and when they find one that feels right they embrace it and retain it without much further questioning. As we have seen, this core belief is often one they learned early in life, based on traditional religious or cultural values.

Which is the better approach? One might argue that the intellectual quest is the more profound, the one more likely to lead to genuine understanding. At the same time, one can lose one's soul in the course of turning one's attention inward and becoming disconnected with the rest of the world. The disadvantage of the leaders' way is that it can result in a superficial, illusory conception of the self, based on borrowed values. On the other hand, it liberates a person's energies and encourages him to act in the world and to add to its complexity. Each approach has its valid place in the scheme of things.

Even though "knowing oneself" may not involve as strenuous a quest for a business leader as it does for a philosopher, it is still an arduous task. It means reflecting seriously on one's own experience, asking: *What are the things that matter most to me? Who are the people I admire most? What kind of person do I definitely not want to be? What are the values I would not compromise under any circumstance?* Or, in the words of Max DePree: "Management has a lot to do with answers. But leadership is a function of questions. And the first question for a leader always is: 'Who do we intend to be?' Not 'What are we going to do?' but 'Who do we intend to be?' "

Knowing oneself is not so much a question of discovering what is present in one's self, but rather of creating who one wants to be. For instance, in Western cultures we are accustomed to thinking of the "self" as an entity bounded by skin and bones. In many Asian and African cultures, however, the self is conceived of as a node in a network of relationships. You think of yourself in terms of your ancestors, parents, siblings, and cousins, extending for generations in the past, like the roots of a tree. You are effectively no one outside the context of this network. Or perhaps you are an *idiot,* which was the Greek word for a person who lived alone, apart from the community that transformed the animal organism into a human being.

The question "Who do I want to be?" is best answered not in terms of the present alone, but with a view toward one's entire life. In many religions, from Tibet to Mesoamerica, the advice of wise men and women has been that one should choose death to be one's counselor. While this may sound like a somewhat macabre idea, it is actually quite liberating. Think of it in terms of instead of being afraid of your death, you ask of it: "Tell me, is this a good idea? Should I take this job, marry this person? When I come to the end of my days, will I be sorry I did this, or glad?" Given that we can't avoid death, we might as well get it to help counsel us while we are alive.

Jane Fonda, who divided her life into three acts, decided after her sixtieth birthday that she was now facing the final act, and came to the following conclusion: "I thought to myself, well if that's the case and if what I'm scared of isn't death, but getting to the end with regrets, then I've got to figure out what would be the things that I would regret when I got to the last act if I hadn't done them or achieved them by then. And they were: having an intimate relationship and having made a difference." In other words, what she hopes to achieve is psychological complexity resulting from differentiation ("making a difference") and integration ("having an intimate relationship").

Developing Strengths, Discovering Opportunities

In creating one's self, it makes sense to build on one's strengths. While the statement, "all men are created equal," is an enlightened political idea, it does not describe the reality of the human condition. Some of us are born with superior physical strength, others with a greater facility to visualize objects in space; some seem able to memorize music without effort and others have a photographic memory for numbers. People who are blessed with a particular gift will typically pursue what comes easily to them.

Often, however, we don't have a good notion of what our talents are, because we have never had a chance to try them out. For instance, John Gardner was a modest college teacher until he was drafted into the army during World War II. In the service he was forced to take on managerial responsibilities, which he discovered fit his talents even better than teaching did. When he returned to civilian life he was given increasingly more demanding administrative jobs, until he was named chairman of the Carnegie Foundation, and then was asked by President Lyndon B. Johnson to serve as the first secretary of health, education, and welfare. He was in his late fifties when he entered the world of Washington politics, where he made another discovery: He liked, and was good at, running a large bureaucracy and at the wheeling and dealing in the Cabinet. This sort of experience, which is by no means rare, convinced Gardner that most of us use only a small part of our natural abilities and may never find out what we are really capable of doing.

Some visionary leaders take stock of their skills rather early in life. Sir John Templeton recalls that in college he was considering becoming a missionary. However, he came to realize that many other young people had equal or greater talents than his in that direction—they were more extroverted and better at preaching and counseling. So instead he decided that his skills were better suited to a different career:

> When I was in college, I examined the talents that God gave me. God gives everybody many, many talents, but not the same ones. And so each of us at some stage ought to examine carefully what talents we have and don't have, so that we can use them to best advantage. And the one that seemed to crystallize when I was at university, was that for the first time in my life I knew people who had investments. But listening to the parents of my classmates, I didn't find any that had investments outside one nation. And to me that seemed

narrow-minded—that surely, you can do a better job if you are searching everywhere instead of just one locality, or one industry.

Having identified what he thought was a challenge he could deal with better than others, he started on the long journey which eventually resulted in the establishment of the first and one of the most successful international investment funds.

Occasionally the discovery of one's calling comes even earlier. In typical Horatio Alger fashion, Christine Comaford Lynch relates how when as a child she was selling lemonade and cupcakes from a case set up on the curb, she realized: "Oh this is fun. This is fun! It's fun to see if you can empty the case by the end of the day, not by eating it." Richard Jacobsen shares an almost identical account:

> I first went into business when I was about ten. My friend and I formed the B&J Beverage Company. We had a wagon and a cooler and we would go down to the Nehi bottling company and buy cases of soda pop. Then we would get ice and put it in our wagon, in the cooler, and put all of these soda pop bottles in the cooler. They were building houses all around us, so we would take our wagon and go from construction project to construction project and sell soda pop to the workers.

But just as often the discovery of how much fun business can be comes after high school, or even later. Some CEOs were attracted to business after professional stints in law, accounting, or engineering. The major factor to consider when taking stock of one's skills is to pay close attention to how it feels to do different things, and to be objective about evaluating one's performance. John Sobrato explains: " I want to be good at what I do. Or I don't do it. I don't play cards because I'm not good at cards. If I don't do something well, I just leave it and go on to something else." Douglas

Yearley was trained as an engineer, and it wasn't until he took a management course at Harvard that he realized he enjoyed business more, and that he could "add more value" by switching: "I realized how much I *loved* the game that was business. . . . I turned out to be a pretty bad engineer, in my judgment. It's a good thing I found business."

It makes little sense to want to be an opera singer if one does not have a suitable voice, or a major league batter if one lacks good eye-hand coordination. It is hardly worthwhile to want to be a physician or a vet if one can't stand the sight of blood. These are obvious conclusions, yet it is amazing how often people ignore realities in pursuit of objectives that are either out of their reach, or that they wouldn't enjoy even if they could reach them.

Anything that we can do well, that we enjoy doing, and that there is a demand for, is worth taking seriously as a skill to develop. But that means one should try to explore as many of one's abilities as possible so as not to miss any hidden potentialities. When asked what advice she would give to a young person who was planning a business career, Anita Roddick replies:

> Well first of all, I wouldn't talk to them like that. I'd say, "Listen, don't even talk about business—don't be controlled by language. Don't even say the word 'business.' Bury it. Talk about livelihood. Talk about a livelihood that you can create for yourself, an honorable livelihood that gives you freedom." So what is the skill that you've got? Maybe you've got a skill and you can mold it into an interest that can create a livelihood. . . . And don't think big, because that's the obsession with this bloody culture. It's always got to be the biggest. Why don't you just be the best or the most creative or the funniest or something?

As some of these quotes suggests, it is difficult to assess challenges and skills in isolation: You need a certain level of skill to recognize a challenging opportunity. Or conversely, if you do well in confronting a particular challenge, that reveals a skill you may have. They are essentially two sides of the same coin.

People who spend most of their lives in apathy and relaxation never notice the opportunities for action that surround them, or if they do, they believe they are not entitled to them. There is a certain fatalistic acceptance of one's place in the scheme of things, so that anything new or untried is perceived as out of one's reach—"that's not for me." This attitude not only blinds one to possibility, but also makes it difficult to discover what one's latent skills might be.

Here is where the traits of curiosity, interest, and openness to experience that are so strong in visionary leaders are especially useful. The more opportunities one is willing to explore, the better chances one has of discovering one's strengths. Early success at learning these strengths has also its downside, because it can result in halting the process of discovery and growth. A manager who is good at dealing with emergencies may become so dependent on having fires to put out that he never proactively develops his own programs or his own vision, and when because of his success he gets promoted to a higher position has no idea what to do. Similarly, if the only challenges a person recognizes are job-related, then when retirement comes her life will become dull and meaningless. To experience flow continuously, one must keep cultivating interest and curiosity, respond to a wide range of opportunities, and develop as many skills as possible.

So one gets to know the self in two different ways. The first is the voyage of discovery of the thinker, the second is the creative ordeal of the man or woman of action. Business leaders usually belong to the second category: They take stock of their personal strengths, their cultural and family background, the possibilities they see around them, and out of all this material they fashion an ideal self. It is the expression of this self that becomes their vision.

Finding Your Place

With very few exceptions—such as independent farmers, artists, and some professionals—most people work in organizations. Ideally it is the organization that will provide the possibilities for action that will provide flow to the worker. There are two main approaches one can take to try to guarantee that the challenges of the workplace will provide a suitable level of challenges to match one's skills. The first or entreprencurial way is to create one's own firm. One of the main attractions of entrepreneurship is precisely this ability to set one's own goals and define the tasks that best suit one's skills.

The second is to search for an already existing environment that fits one's talents. Keep in mind that finding a job should never be just a matter of finding a source of income. The organization you work for will shape your entire identity. It will either enable you to grow or stunt you; it will either energize you or drain you; it will strengthen your values or make you cynical. Sobrato advises: "Go to work for somebody that will take time to guide you along, and somebody that's recognized as being a leader in their profession."

Many people enter their first job still unsure of what they want to be and of their skills, and it is their experience at work during this period that is likely to determine the direction in which they will go professionally. Anita Roddick's advice is typical:

> Look for your passion. What makes you excited? What turns you on? . . . Go towards companies that you really like, really admire. . . . What do you admire about them? Spend, if you can, an internship there, or just knock on the door and say: "Hey, can I work here for cheap?" . . . Find organizations that move your spirit if you can. Work alongside them. . . . and have fun. There's so much

fun to be had. . . . When you spend ninety-five percent
of your life in a work environment, it can't be dour.

If the first job doesn't work out, or if it becomes stale, it is better to resume the search than continue in a dead-end situation.
Sir John Templeton remarks:

> The first advice is to survey the field and decide who is
> the most advanced, who is the most respected, and try
> to get a job with them. . . . You should not think that
> your first choice is always going to be the right choice.
> You should always be studying and asking where else in
> the whole world, not just in one nation, where else
> in the whole world are my talents needed. You don't say
> to yourself, "This is going to be my lifetime career." You
> say, "I'm going to start here, but continually I'm going
> to be studying all over the world where it is I can do
> more good."

At first glance these two suggestions seem almost contrary.
Anita Roddick bases her decision on passion and fun, while Templeton speaks the language of the Puritan ethic—where will my
God-given talents be best used? But at a deeper level the advice is
the same. Both leaders are urging: Find a place where you can
function at 100 percent, where your values and skills will have a
chance to be fully expressed. In other words an environment with
soul, where work can be flow.

The Mastery of Consciousness

One often meets extremely competent people, including successful CEOs of great companies, who are perfectly conscious as they
make billion-dollar decisions, yet who are not fully in control of
their consciousness. They act more or less by rote, following old

habits and responding to familiar cues. Even though their power strikes fear in the hearts of thousands, they have lost the ability to make their own choices. They have become part of a program that dictates their actions—to increase shareholder value, market share, brand visibility. Their psychological complexity has been arrested: What they do, think, and feel has become predictable and routine.

It is all too easy to become trapped under the glass ceiling of a job and to stop growing. To be able to experience flow throughout life, it is necessary to become the master of one's psychic energy. Warren Bennis calls "management of the self" a leadership commandment, one that is necessary to keep both the manager and the organization healthy. From the point of view of flow theory, the most crucial aspects of self-management are learning to align attention, time, and habits with one's vision for the self.

Attention. In Chapter 4 we have seen that how much one can experience in a lifetime is limited by the amount of information the brain can process. We shape our lives by deciding what to pay attention to, and by how long and how intensely to do so. Because attention is what makes things happen in consciousness, it is useful to think of it as psychic energy. For some people attention is directed from the outside, by stimuli like external emergencies and the demands of work and family. Others direct their psychic energy guided by goals and values that they have simply taken from their cultural environment without reflection. Those who have followed the advice to "know thyself" direct their energies on the basis of values they have chosen to adopt only after careful consideration of their suitability and value.

When asked what she believed made her a successful businesswoman, Christine Comaford Lynch first mentions her "intuition." Then she corrects herself: "It's not just intuition—but it comes from paying attention! The more we pay attention—I get distracted, definitely, I like doing twenty million things at once, and I should probably do three at once instead of twenty million, so paying attention is huge." As we have seen we can at most realistically do two or three things at once, and this only if we keep shifting very quickly from one task to another; so while it seems as if we are doing them simultaneously, in actuality we are performing them serially. Still, the point Comaford Lynch is making is valid and noteworthy. It is the direction of our attention and its intensity that will determine what we accomplish, and how well.

We usually pay attention to the things we like, that interest us, that engage our skills. But the relationship works the other way, as well: We get to like whatever we pay careful attention to. Because of this, a good strategy is to invest energy in things that have the potential to sustain growth, even if at first we are not particularly interested in them. Eventually, as we learn more about them, interest will be awakened. One area for fertile engagement is the specific details of a project. When asked what accounts for his success in business, Sobrato replies:

> Attention to detail. I am very detail-oriented. If I'm doing a project, I really get involved with all the little details that make our project stand out from others. If I'm negotiating, I think I can negotiate ad nauseam on little details, because I enjoy that sort of thing.

The great modernist architect Mies van der Rohe once quipped that "God is in the details." What he may have meant is that close attention to the details of any task brings about the deep concentration of flow, and in that state one feels temporarily as if one were living on a different, more exalted plane of existence.

Like anything else, the management of attention requires being able to balance extremes. Some people have such a narrow range of interests that they don't notice most of what's happening around them. They may become very proficient at their specialty, but the world in which they live is so restricted that sooner or later they end up exhausting the opportunities it offers. Other people squander their psychic energy wantonly, noticing everything and following hundreds of loose ends, without getting to know any subject thoroughly, or achieving mastery of any one skill.

One way to avoid these extremes is the strategy used by Linus Pauling, the Nobel-Prize winner in Chemistry and Peace, who described his use of psychic energy as follows:

> I have a picture, a sort of general theory of the universe in my mind that I have built up over the decades. If I read an article, or hear someone give a seminar talk, or in some other way get some piece of information about science that I hadn't had before, I ask myself: "How does that fit into my picture of the universe?" and if it doesn't fit, I ask: "Why doesn't it fit in?"

Pauling's is a good account of how a complex consciousness functions: You start out with a "general theory" (or core value, or vision) that is developed over time; then you integrate into it all relevant information, whether it supports or challenges the theory. In this way one keeps growing from a stable base, ever expanding a circle of connections while maintaining a unique perspective.

Time. Attention and time are two different aspects of the same underlying process: Mastering one's attention involves mastering time, and vice versa. If you learn how much psychic energy you need to invest in a project, or a game of golf, then you don't have to worry about how to use time, because by solving the first equation you will have also solved the second. Business leaders are aware of the finitude of time and its relation to the tasks one wishes to accomplish. They would all agree with Christine Comaford Lynch: "The most precious gift is time, because there's definitely a limited amount. You don't have as much time usually as you think you do—you don't know when your number's up in the great 'deli of life.' "

Richard Jacobsen has his own personal image to describe the time crunch we all experience:

> Time comes in blobules, and time blobules are cannibalistic by nature. Institutionally driven blobules are relatively more cannibalistic than other blobules. You have to take care of how you manage your time blobules.

Ironically, advances in technology that were supposed to save us time often add to the pressure instead. Christine Comaford Lynch comments on the latest manifestation of this trend, and suggests how important it is to learn to master it, instead of becoming its captive:

> How has technology influenced the business world? You know I'd love to say that it's helped us out but I don't think it has as much as enabled us to work all the time. You know, that's the bummer. Now we have e-mail, we take our PCs home, now we work all the time. So, I think it's good though. It helps you to a degree. It helps you decide to become more human or to become one of those people who has no hobbies, has no outside life, all they can think about is work.

We tend to allocate time, just as we invest attention, to the kind of activities we enjoy doing. People who love their work end up spending more and more time on the job, to the exclusion of less exciting pursuits, like spending time with family or reflecting on the purpose of their lives. Many complain about not having enough time for their home life, but in truth this is a choice they have made, usually unconsciously, because work produces more flow than anything else they could be doing. As Orit Gadiesh admits:

> There are times when I feel I work too much. But basically people make choices that they enjoy, and so when I

find myself feeling that way, I must admit I made the choice. It is absolutely that I made a choice. And I am probably enjoying aspects of that—even though I may not be doing something else that I would also like to do.

What is key here is to define one's priorities, and then abide by them. Mike Murray is a man determined to stick by his guns:

> The contract that I've always had with myself is this: I'll work as hard as I can work on the job, then I'm also going to go home and have my family and personal life. And if that's not good enough for the company they have a choice. The choice is, they can ask me to leave. But I'm never going to win the award for the person who put in the longest hours on the job. And I can't let my ego feel bad about that, because I've chosen a different yardstick that I'm going to run my life by.

Jack Greenberg, like many of his peers, has tried to develop a strategy to achieve the elusive balance between work and family life:

> I had a partner that I worked for once, when I was complaining about not being home enough, who said that the way you do this is that you treat your family as your most important client, so that you make time for them. And then make sure that the time you're spending with them is quality time. So you're not just there—reading the paper, and don't bother me—but you're actually engaged, as you would be with a client.

The problem with this tactic is that in dealing with a client the parameters are well defined: the goals are clear, feedback is quick, and skills are generally matched to opportunities. In other words, the conditions for flow are present. At home, on the other hand, the situation is much more ambiguous: Spouse and children have their own agendas, and differences in ages and backgrounds of family members make it difficult to focus on the same topics—with the result that much of the effort seems a huge waste of time. Not surprisingly, it becomes easier and more attractive to put one's energies where they seem to have the greatest effect, and that usually means work. If one is serious about family life, however, one must also take on the challenge of transforming it into a flow experience—which means investing as much psychic energy into it as one would in making a business organization work.

In many cases, even when our bodies are at home, our minds are not. Attention remains focused on work-related problems, and our family quickly notices that we are mentally and emotionally absent. Mike Markkula of Apple developed a successful strategy to avoid this situation, which consisted of seeing to it that the job did not claim all his psychic energy:

> So I started using a little technique that I developed. When the car door shuts to leave the plant and drive home, I am going to start thinking about what is important at home. It's hard to do because you have all of this stuff from work popping in! But if you concentrate on it for a half an hour on the way home, by the time . . . you walk in the door you say, how did the such and such go that you went to today? And you are actually interested because you are back in this other world!

Deborah Besemer offers another tactic to keep the balance between work and family:

> The rules that I live by are: Do not work on weekends. And that's really hard in a start-up. There's lots and lots of work to do. I won't come into the office on the weekends. I will take my PC home, I will get up really early

in the morning before everybody else and work on it and then when the kids get up I shut it off. When I have to fly out to a meeting and people say, "Gee why don't you come in the night before for dinner?" I say "No I won't come up the night before for dinner," I'll get up at four o'clock in the morning, take the first flight out in the morning so I can be there for the beginning of the meeting, but can at least be [home to] put my kids to bed.

Another consequence of getting overly caught up in one's work is that any "waste" of time becomes intolerably painful. In the years I have been counseling midlevel executives, I have been struck by how the most frequently mentioned personal trait the managers wished they could change was "impatience." What did they mean by it, I wondered? The examples poured forth in an endless stream: "I can't wait for my subordinates to finish a sentence. I know what they are going to say, and I don't want to wait for them to babble on." "It seems such a waste of time to read my grandchildren the same stupid stories I used to read to my children." "I hate going out to dinner. You sit in this ritzy French restaurant, and kill a couple of hours watching waiters scraping crumbs off the tablecloth. For what? I would be happier eating pizza at home watching the news on TV." "I am just getting more and more short-tempered with people who are not up to speed."

Mike Hackworth's description is typical:

I had an enormous impatience for people who couldn't *get* what we were trying to do, real quick. And so I'd get angry and just extremely agitated, and then I began to realize that there's a distribution of people in this world, and what you really need to do unless you're just going to go off with a few people is that you've got to be able to accommodate a variety of attitudes, intellects and what have you, and so that was kind of an enlightening experience, a maturity thing, that came along when I was maybe in my midtwenties.

William Pollard describes a similar scenario:

> I think at times I can be too impatient with incompetence. I think the times I feel like I've really failed is in interpersonal relationships . . . [I may have been] right in the decision, but wrong in the way the [other] person was confronted as part of that right decision. . . . Whenever you're in a relationship with another person, and you need to reach a decision, if the other person doesn't agree with you, [and they feel that] they either have to fight you right to the end or just simply fold, then . . . you haven't done the job right.

These managers understood that their impatience made them less effective—it alienated the people with whom they worked and offended their spouses and children. They knew that to do their job well, they had to come to recognize other people as individuals with personal needs and quirks, and not treat them as if they were negligible robots whose only significance lay in what they could contribute to a project—and in the shortest amount of time. Yet they still found it almost impossible to become more patient. As Max DePree says, "One of the problems people have is if you think you can figure things out . . . we become very impatient with people who can't. That really ruins relationships. I had to have help in understanding that." When too much psychic energy has been invested in the job, the value of work will grow in one's mind to the point it overshadows everything else. Ultimately, chronic impatience also begins to impact negatively on business decisions. Christine Comaford Lynch explains:

> When things screw up is when you feel too much urgency. That the start-up is like, "If you don't give me this

bridge loan, I'm going to go to somebody else." And you're like, this seems like a really hot deal, maybe I should do this. So when you're not still, and checking and taking the time, that's when you mess up. 'Cause you're letting somebody else's agenda pressure you. And what I've learned now is, "Go somewhere else. I need more time. This is what our time line is. I need this time."

Jack Greenberg also uses a similar delaying tactic to allow more time to himself, referring to the importance of what in creativity research is called "incubation"—the subliminal parallel-processing activity that takes place in the mind when we are not consciously trying to solve a problem:

I also find that if I'm not sure about what to do, if I just take a couple of days to reflect on it, somehow—even if it's not conscious—I come to a clearer understanding of the problem by just not forcing myself to make a decision that minute. It just internalizes. I don't know how to explain it. . . . But I think some of it is subconscious. Your brain must be working on stuff that you're not thinking about. Oftentimes it comes back with some clarity.

Despite much helpful advice that has been developed about the best way to manage one's time, in my own experience there is no one best way: What works for one person may not for another. There are some very successful leaders whose every minute is scheduled months in advance, and others equally successful who like to keep their schedule as flexible as possible to take advantage of unforeseen opportunities. Some people work best by taking care of easy decisions early in the day, so as to have the time to focus on the important matters later; others prefer to tackle the major issues first and then coast along addressing the simpler problems afterward. Whatever your habits, it's important to pay attention to your own rhythm: What works best for you? If you enjoy being tightly scheduled and dealing with priorities first, then it's likely that you will do your best work under those conditions. It makes sense, therefore, to build the most flow-producing rhythm into the way you use time at work. And the same holds for those working under you: There is no reason why every person on the team should be marching to the same tune.

Habits. As one's attention keeps being invested along the same lines, habits are formed. Aristotle recognized that virtues are the result of habits developed over time, and the great early American psychologist William James wrote that habits are the most important components of human psychology. The truth of this statement becomes apparent if one reflects on the fact that our lives are the result of where and how we have invested attention over the years, and that this in turn is based on what we learned to pay attention to earlier in life. It is impossible to do justice to this enormous topic in these pages, but at least a few issues relevant to it are worth considering.

What sort of habits one develops depends primarily on two factors: first, on discipline and character—that is, on hard work; and second, on what one enjoys doing. Ideally, one should enjoy learning the kinds of pursuits that lead to growth in complexity. (This is the process of psychological capital formation discussed in Chapter 4.) If a person has reached adulthood only enjoying activities like watching television, partying, gambling, or drugs, chances are that he is not going to be much good at anything else. In this way the pattern of energy investment learned in the early years has momentous consequences for the rest of one's life.

Still, new habits can be set at any time—even in old age. As one comes to notice that certain ways of thinking or doing things are not as effective as others, one can build better strategies into one's repertoire of behaviors. Here, for instance, Jack Greenberg describes one of these changes in strategy:

Another thing I've learned is that you don't make an important decision when your own mental attitude isn't in a healthy state. Because you're prone to make a bad decision. You've got to make sure you're not too tired or not down, you're not depressed—whatever the words are—because it affects your thought processes.

Because religion is so strong a core value in many lives, prayer can become an important habit that serves to get one in touch with one's soul and set one's bearings for the future. Sir John Templeton describes how he integrates regular prayers in his daily activities:

I pray a lot, and naturally, if I pray—as I mentioned earlier, I try to do two or three things at once—if I pray while I'm driving, for example, I find that it's easier to pray a prayer that I prayed several times before than to think up a new one, you see. So I do, to a large extent, pray prayers that I have designed years ago. But at the same time I'm always trying to find different and better ways.

Aaron Feuerstein of Malden Mills describes vividly how self-chosen, enjoyable habits can restore vigor and enthusiasm late in life, even when to an outsider they may seem obsessively strenuous:

I am up at five-fifteen every day. I do one hour of exercise. One day running, the other day calisthenics. One hour. Not fifty-nine minutes. One hour, one hour, one hour . . . At the same time that I do the physical exercise, I try to do mental exercises. I memorize an hour's worth of Hebrew poetry when I run, and an hour of English poetry when I'm doing calisthenics. And so I feel I am doing justice not only to my body but to my brain as well. And when I am done I am exhausted, but I have gotten so that I can come into the mill and not be exhausted. . . . I'm ready for the challenge.

Richard Jacobsen, who is a member of the Church of Latter-day Saints, follows a similar practice: "Every morning I read the scriptures, and pray, and write in my journals for about an hour or an hour and a half."

When habits are not as thoroughly routinized as the ones described above, it helps to set aside specific times for reflection, to take stock of where one has been and where one wants to be next. This can be done each day, or as seldom as a few times a year. Christine Comaford Lynch describes her life-planning practice:

> It's a sitting down with my journal, and it's usually in June and December, it just works out that way. Okay. Is my life working? And there's a lot of aspects to that. Is my career life working? Is my personal life working? Am I stretching enough? What am I afraid of? Where can I go to get to the next level? Am I progressing spiritually? Am I still feeling close to God or am I getting swept up in stuff and, sliding? Yeah. I think it's so easy just to get swept up in stuff and then to wake up a few years later and go, "Whoa, where did my life go?" So yeah, I really think it's important to assess. Hugely, hugely important.

To answer such questions accurately, however, requires forming the habit of paying attention to one's feelings and actions on a daily basis. This returns us to the point made at the beginning of this chapter: To know oneself is the first step toward making flow a part of one's entire life. But just as there is no free lunch in the material economy, nothing comes free in the psychic one. If one is not willing to invest psychic energy in the internal reality of consciousness, and instead squanders it in chasing external rewards, one loses mastery of one's life, and ends up becoming a puppet of circumstances.

Chapter 9

The Future of Business

Will Business Survive?

I n every historical period people occupying certain key social
roles achieve a position of supremacy over the rest of the
population. Depending on the means of production and the
values of society, it is either hunters, warriors, priests, landowners
or merchants that end up running not only the economy but also
politics and culture. They accumulate wealth, influence the laws,
and even set the standards of truth and beauty. It is fairly obvious
that in our time the most powerful segment of society is the one
engaged in business; it not only controls the flow of resources,
from food to oil, but also has a disproportionate voice in how the
country is run, and by whom.

Business interests dictate American interventions abroad,
whether to protect investments in the banana groves of Latin
America or in the oil fields of Kuwait. The most important functions of society, which used to be relatively independent of the
market, have now become servants of Wall Street. From managed
health care to agribusiness, from the media to genetic research,
from education to music and entertainment, the intrinsic value of
these institutions has been overshadowed by their valuation on the
market. It no longer matters whether a newspaper does an excellent job in providing useful information; if it does not ring the

cash register at the expected rate, it's deemed a failure. It does not matter if a hospital serves the health of the community well; what counts is whether its dividends meet the investors' expectations. And the profits margins that are expected, which used to be in the single digits, have now escalated into the twenties.

Of course it is not the fault of business alone that we have arrived at this juncture. It is society as a whole that has developed excessive greed, a taste for the highest possible returns on investment in the shortest possible amount of time. In the past, people didn't expect that all their happiness would be provided by the market. Our ancestors took pride in their jobs, drew security from land and livestock, placed hope in religion, and were comforted by family and community. The small incremental wealth brought by financial investments was considered just a part of a widely diversified portfolio of blessings. But now it seems that to cultivate job, religion, family, and community takes too much effort; it is much easier simply to wait for our stocks to miraculously multiply. Managers in publicly held companies can do little to stem this tide of expectations; they know that if they implement a strategy that yields less profit in order to optimize some other value, some sharp-eyed investor will ask for their dismissal at the next stock-holders' meeting.

In these market conditions businessmen who aim higher than merely generating profits face an uphill struggle. Yet with power and leadership comes a burden of social responsibility. In the past, when people began to suspect that the Church was not adding much value to their lives, its legitimacy began to decline and so did its power. When the landed aristocracy in Europe was perceived to be a hindrance to the well-being of the population as a whole, its decline was inevitable. Similarly business will not succeed in retaining its hegemony, if it turns out that the market comes to be widely perceived as just a convenience for the benefit of the few, which does not contribute to the happiness of the many.

The business leaders interviewed in our study were generally somewhat ambivalent about their historical role. On the one hand, they were unanimously positive about the contribution their work was making to society. Occasionally they adopted a tone of enthusiastic boosterism: "Successful businesses really build the nation's economy. Business builds the American dream; that's what business does. Business pays the taxes; business builds careers; business fuels ambition; business builds the houses; business builds the highways because it all comes from business. And business is what attracts people to come to this country. . . . Business pays for advances in education; advances in health; advances in technology. Business is what makes the United States what it is."

Likewise, our subjects were generally quite optimistic about the direction in which business was heading. They all claimed that business practices are more ethical now than they have ever been before. There is both more transparency and accountability as well as a greater concern for the welfare of employees, the community, and the environment. Although all of them admitted that they knew some callous and unethical colleagues, they were adamant that these were exceptions, and that there is no greater proportion of unscrupulous individuals in business than there is, for example, in academia or among the clergy.

Of course, one would expect such a favorable assessment from members of a fraternity of businesspeople. Not only is understandable self-interest involved, but, as we have seen in Chapter 7, these are individuals who are temperamentally optimistic in most matters. One does not survive long in the boardroom or on the golf course by being critical of the business enterprise.

On the other hand, despite this overall approving judgment, visionary leaders are also aware that there are severe problems that need to be addressed for business to continue to uphold its share of the implicit social contract with the rest of society. One of the most often mentioned troubling issues is the growing inequality in the system of rewards. Here is how Douglas Yearley characterizes the dilemma: "The negative is we get an increasing spread between the most talented and the least talented and what their compensation is. . . . There's too much greed. The score card is how much money do you have or are you worth?" J. Irwin Miller takes up the same issue:

> And an example of [the problem] is the terribly high levels of pay that some CEOs go and fight for, at a time when general wages are not rising at all. I think this is an invitation to some kind of social unrest sooner or later. The difference between the top and the bottom person in most organizations is now greater—I'm referring to their pay—than it ever has been.
>
> . . . Too many of these young people that we get out of business schools, their major aim is to say, "Well, I want to make a million dollars before I am thirty." They don't say, "I want to do a good job or help build a company or something like that." There's nothing much selfless in them, and they're doomed to failure if there isn't a high selfless quality in their own values, if they can't identify with the university or with a corporation or with whatever they're in and say, "I want to help build that outfit." But to express their own values in terms of dollars is probably a failure.

When asked whether he believes that business practices have become better or worse during his own working life, Max DePree also points to the increasing inequity and greed as the darkest clouds on the horizon:

> I think there are always going to be . . . a certain amount of unethical practices in business, and we're not going to control that, and if we've got some laws that help with that, that's fine. My own feeling is that what's more dangerous to the free market system is uncontrolled inequities. One example is . . . what I think are totally unreasonable amounts of money that CEOs are taking out of companies. That comes back to, what is it fair to

ask the customer to pay? There are some things that customers shouldn't have to pay for if all they want to buy is a chair or a car. You know? If I want to buy an SUV, I don't think I ought to pay for the CEO to have an apartment in Zurich where he keeps a mistress. I don't think that ought to be in the price of the car.

It is remarkable to hear successful capitalists express sentiments like the following: "I don't believe that the unfettered free market is going to lead to anything but trouble. You have powerful consumers, and you have powerful manufacturers and suppliers, so you are going to need the government as an intelligent umpire to keep one of them from eating the other one up." Anita Roddick takes the indictment of greed one step further, pointing out the dark side of globalization, which is causing on a worldwide scale the kind of dislocation that the Industrial Revolution brought to countries like England and Germany two and a half centuries ago:

> When you see the huge compensation packages of CEOs, the downsizing which is seen as good business practice, and whole communities just disappearing because of that, and when you see this consistent obsession with going towards countries where they have the most passive and docile workers because the wage structure is different—there's no protection, [especially] to the women workers. I think it alienates humanity in every way. . . . The entire message I have is to try and bring these values of the church and the temple and the great philosophers, whatever they are, and just [include] them as part of the language of business.

This last quote points out one of the dangers that comes with hegemonic power. It suggests that the success of business might enable it to spread and to take over our entire lives, like vigorous cancer cells that devour the healthy organs of the body. In that scenario the only measure of value will be financial success, and the only good that which increases profit. Long-range plans will be shelved for short-term profits. Loyalty will be traded at market value. Air, water, and health will be allocated according to the laws of supply and demand. It is precisely to avoid this grim one-dimensional future that the language of business must include the "values of church and temple and the great philosophers."

Unfortunately these values are all too easily forgotten in the normal conduct of business. After all, constant challenges must be met, and the day-to-day operations of any one company appear to have only the most tenuous effect on the ultimate well-being of humankind. By the narrow measure of instant success that we have grown accustomed to, one is likely to do better by ignoring long-term consequences. Yet if business continues to be oblivious to the responsibilities attached to the power it has acquired, sooner or later the immune system of society is going to reject the free-market paradigm.

One solution to this dilemma is to confront more directly the consequences of a purely market-driven view of the world, a course that would involve some guided reflection. As William Pollard comments:

> I don't think we've encouraged leaders to reflect. I think we've encouraged leaders to do. It starts with the educational process. I mentioned in the book [*The Soul of the Firm*] an experience I had at another public company, where I was on a committee responsible for interviewing the next CEO of that company. We were interviewing a lot of candidates. We wanted to somehow figure out what the person's philosophy of life was, whether they were reflective and thinking people. And there's all kinds of ways you can get at that. You can ask them what they read or what they don't read, and so forth. But we

decided to get at it by simply asking this question of every candidate: How do you determine whether something is right or wrong? And we got all kinds of different answers. First of all, most of them thought we were talking about how do you determine whether something is right or wrong in the running of a business. How do you anticipate a problem, or something like that. So, that was the first response. We said, "No, we're not talking about that. We're talking about moral issues." Why is it right to be truthful? Why was it right twenty years ago to think that women could do only certain types of jobs and men had to do every other kind of job? Why was that right? Why is it wrong today? Is it wrong today because the law says it's wrong? Or was it fundamentally wrong and it just wasn't recognized? And what are the new issues? What are the issues in front of us right now that we ought to be thinking about—what is right and what is wrong in the way we conduct business, in the way we treat people? I could get into the environmental issues. I could get into all other issues. What's driving a leader to anticipate those issues? Can the corporation be a moral community for the development of people in addition to producing goods and services? That's a fundamental question. Well, if it can be a moral community, then where is the leadership in thinking through the issue of these standards?

Would it make a difference in the overall business environment if all candidates for leadership positions in business had to explain to search committees their conception of what is right and what is wrong, and what constitutes the foundations of a moral community? It would probably be a valuable first step, but it would have to be followed up with devising measures of success, promotion, and reward that took into account these moral imperatives. Unfortunately, it is all too easy to profess responsibility without actually performing in a responsible way. The popes called themselves "Servant of the servants of God" while amassing vast treasure in the midst of widespread poverty, just as feudal lords styled themselves protectors of widows and orphans while exercising their droit du seigneur. Hypocrisy corrupts more than mere oblivion does.

Those who do take the time to pause and reflect tend to come up with conclusions similar to the one reached by Max DePree:

> I think that my business career was a kind of a pilgrimage, away from, you know—how can you build up the revenues and what is the best you can do with earnings per share?—towards a goal of figuring out, what really are the preserving principles of the free-market system in a democracy? I don't in my heart believe that either a democracy or the free-market system can survive unless we understand what the preserving principles are, and we honor them. Speaking historically, we're very, very young. And we're showing a lot of the marks in the free-market system of attitudes and practices that do not encourage survival of the system.

The Principles of Good Business

What we have learned from these visionary leaders are some concrete notions about how to conduct good business—how to run organizations that make a reasonable profit, but above all else contribute to human happiness and well-being. From their many years of work experience—which cumulatively would stretch back to the Middle Ages and beyond—one can begin to trace outlines of the foundations on which a good business can be built. Of their many ideas, I will choose only three major ones, which seem to be both the most essential and the most widely endorsed.

A Vision Beyond the Self

We have seen that perhaps the most important distinguishing trait of visionary leaders is that they believe in a goal that benefits not only themselves, but others as well. It is such a vision that attracts the psychic energy of other people, and makes them willing to work beyond the call of duty for the organization. In Chapter 7 I called this kind of vision "soul," because it is what transforms workers from self-centered, static individuals into entities yearning to grow and connect with other beings.

But the word "vision" is not quite adequate, for it connotes a visual or mental image of what a leader intends to achieve. The interviews suggest, rather, that what drives them is something more visceral than a mental image. It also involves feelings, and a sense of physical rootedness in a field of forces that includes the self, but is much larger. It is almost as if, instead of being transient visitors on this planet, they feel that they have a permanent place in the cosmos; a unique place that involves specific responsibilities—it is, in other words, a personal destiny, a calling. Such a vision is a powerful device. At the very least, it saves its owner a great amount of psychic energy—he need not spend time debating his actions or his movements, for the road ahead is straight and clear. In times of crisis, when danger and doubt may paralyze others, one possessed of a strong vision is not deterred from the task.

There are three main types of calling that motivate these leaders. The first is simply *to do one's best*. Whether it is Yvon Chouinard's desire to manufacture shirts that are indestructible, or Norman Augustine's determination to build the best aerospace company in the world, the drive to excel is a potent force, one that can become contagious and keep an entire organization focused. Doing one's best is also the spur that leads to creativity, the urge to go beyond the limits of the possible. It is the cutting edge of evolution.

What is imperative to realize is that every individual has the option to do his best. Excellence is not a goal to which only multibillion dollar firms can aspire. When Chouinard first had his vision of making the best climbing equipment in the world, he was a semi-employed blacksmith with only a broken-down station wagon to his name. Anita Roddick was a housewife with no money, credit, or experience when she decided to make and market organic cosmetic products that were body friendly. The list of entrepreneurs who started with no material means but a strong vision is endless—from Henry Ford to Hewlett and Packard, from Ross Perot to Bill Gates. It was not financing that made them successful, but an idea of how to do things better than they were being done.

In fact, creativity is an endless source of innovation—there is always a better way to do something. It is also a very democratic process: One need not be wealthy, well connected, or even well educated to come up with a good new idea. Whether one runs a pizza franchise or a biotech company, the potential for improvement is always present. Building a vision on excellence is open to anyone who wants to do good business.

The second main form of calling is based on *helping people.* Here the leader's sense of responsibility is not focused primarily on coming up with an improved product or service, but on the task of aiding employees, customers, suppliers, and the community in general lead a better life. Of course this goal is not necessarily contrary to wanting to do one's best. Both are often present simultaneously, but usually the priority lies in either one or the other direction.

The leaders agree that while technical competence offers a great advantage, the ability to establish and nurture relationships within the organization is even more essential. As Timothy Rowe points out: "If somebody is focused on long-term success, then they are focused on relationships: They are focused on being reliable, following through. Most relationships are based on honesty." For some leaders there is nothing more critical than to feel that their actions are beneficial to other people, and it is this altruism that makes their leadership effective. Jack Greenberg says: ". . . my interest in people and my enjoyment of the relationships and the value of those relationships—having a point of view about how people ought to be treated—has helped in my career generally, to be more effective as a manager and as a leader."

As with excellence, the goal of being of service to others is an inexhaustible source of inspiration. There is always an opportunity to improve the lives of those with whom one works, or of those who use the products or services one provides. It yields an endlessly satisfying objective, whether one does it for the love of God, Buddha, or because of a fundamental belief that all human beings are worth the effort.

And then there is the calling *to build a better world*. Some of our subjects have developed a sense of responsibility that reaches out to the community in which they work, to democracy as the best upholder of civic institutions, and to the environment that allows us to survive and prosper. Most of them pursue this aspect of their calling outside the workplace, by devoting psychic energy and funding to various nonprofit ventures. But some leaders manage to take on this global responsibility as a strategic goal of their organization. When that happens, business truly acquires soul.

When each of these three elements of vision—concern for excellence, for people, and for the wider environment—are present, business is transformed from a tool for making profits into a creative, humane experiment for improving life. Clearly, making profits also improves life to the extent that shareholders benefit financially. But to reduce the goals of business to merely financial returns—which we know do not enhance appreciably the quality of life—that benefit only a select number of owners, with only the minimum legal concern for the consequences of one's operations, is to sell short its powerful potential. For business to really contribute to the common welfare, and thus assure its own survival through the support of society, it will need to nurture a greater number of visionary leaders who can infuse soul in their organizations, and who can convince the rest of us that it is worth investing in their projects, even if their rate of return falls below the level of our dreams.

How Good Businesses Operate

But vision alone is not enough, for it has to be translated into the operating practices of the institution. Lofty goals that are not eventually implemented lead to cynicism and hypocrisy. What did we learn from these leaders about how to "walk the walk" in managing good business?

Probably the most important principle of organizational behavior that emerged from the interviews was the importance of *trust*, which is brought about by *respect*. Any group of people working toward a common goal is held together by a combination of two motives: self-interest and common interest. The former can be bought by external incentives: pay, promotion, prestige. The latter motive, common interest, must be earned through a demonstration of respect for the value of the members of the team. Workers will not place themselves at the service of a leader's vision unless they feel that the rules of the organization are fairly applied, that their contribution is recognized, and that their integrity is respected.

To achieve this end, managers must invest a great deal of their psychic energy in monitoring and enhancing the well-being of the group. And before all else, they have to develop self-discipline based on self-knowledge, which will prevent them from acting capriciously and selfishly. Whenever a leader cuts corners, shows favoritism, is unfair or thoughtless he undermines the common interest of the group. If this happens often enough, the only motive keeping the organization coherent will be self-interest. This not only lowers morale but increases the operating costs of the organization, because a greater amount of extrinsic incentives will be needed to keep people performing their tasks. Robert Shapiro describes what it takes for a leader to establish a common basis of trust:

I don't really believe in traditional power in large organizations, because I don't think it works very well. You
can't walk around and say: "Aha! I saw you say something that wasn't true. You're fired." It's just not possible. . . . You are in a position to start conversations. You
are in a position to influence what people will talk about
and think about. And from that point on, what effect it
has is a direct function of the quality of the conversations you've initiated. It either resonates with people,
appeals to something that matters to them, or it doesn't.
It either feels authentic to them and feels like something they genuinely want to engage in, or it doesn't.
And there's no way of compelling it. It's an invitation.

The "invitation" that Shapiro describes is a time-consuming,
open-ended process, and one that lacks the clarity of the old
command-and-control mode of operation. Genghis Khan, for one,
would have been appalled by it. Nevertheless, it is the only way to
shape a group of people held together by organic solidarity, by
common purpose. Such a group will be largely self-organizing,
and open to the future—an evolving organism rather than a
closed system. When such a group of people works together freely
on a common task, the bonds that arise can produce a tremen-
dously satisfying feeling of community. Shapiro does not hesitate
to call it love:

. . . [T]here seems to be a pretty widespread longing to
have work that's on a "no bullshit" basis, to have work
that's real, that counts, that matters for people, and to
be in a place where you care about the folks around you
and know that they care about you. That really is a longing. . . . and this is something that's a real taboo to talk
about—that there were many circumstances in the business world in which people genuinely loved each other.
As I say, it's not discussible, but there's just no other way

to describe it. . . . and it's not a coincidence that, at least
as I see it, that also is the environment that is most likely
to produce extraordinary achievement and extraordinary financial performance.

Beyond providing respect and a sense of common purpose, an
organization that does good business is also *concerned with the personal growth of its members.* An evolving system is not static but tends
toward complexity. The most obvious expression of this concern is
providing opportunities for life-long education. As C. William Pollard points out:

> The other thing that's occurring is that business will pro-
> vide the primary vehicle for continuous learning. The
> idea that a certain part of our lives we can go to school
> and learn, and then other parts of our lives we can go to
> work and work, the difference between school and
> work, that line is blurring.

But it is not just technical learning that's at issue. Given the fact
that adults spend the bulk of their life at their workplace, an organization that does not enable its members to grow as people—to
grow in self-knowledge, in wisdom, and in the ability to relate to
others—is not doing them any favors. What is needed is the kind
of workplace Robert Shapiro describes: "under the right circumstances, people could integrate . . . within themselves and learn
about themselves, could grow, develop, could connect within the
context of a for-profit business organization." In contrast, a business that ignores the complexity of human beings—ignores their
need for love as well as growth—and that only deals with employees as cogs in the process of production, ends up diminishing
them.

The best way management can help motivate workers to pursue
common goals and grow in the process of doing so, is by *providing
opportunities for flow in the workplace.* Assuming that an appealing

vision has been communicated, and trust established, then what remains to be done is to make certain that organizational behavior does not deprive workers of the enjoyment that comes naturally from being able to do one's best. To summarize briefly the essential conditions for flow to occur, they are: clear goals that can be adapted to meet changing conditions; immediate feedback to one's actions; and a matching of the challenges of the job with the worker's skills. A book could be written on each of these three simple requirements, which have been described more fully in Chapters 3 and 4. When the goals are clear and the challenges high but attainable the workplace can become as exciting as the final game of the World Series and as soulful as a religious revival. Shapiro describes this feeling:

> [M]y predecessor in this job used to go around asking people, "What was the best experience you ever had while you were working here?" And they always talk about some kind of crisis—the flood is coming and we have to protect the plant, or a customer called and said they were going to cancel the order unless we could hit some standard we never hit before. Whatever. Some challenge that's really difficult, maybe impossible, and there's usually limited time to deal with it and it's way beyond the capabilities that people thought they had. And for a period of time they forget all the rules. Everyone tells the same story. It doesn't matter what the crisis was, the stories are always the same. It'll be, "Well, we worked really hard and we kind of forgot whose job was what. We just all did it, and the best ideas came from very unlikely places, from people who institutionally were thought to be incapable of having ideas. And we really did a terrific job.". . . And they all felt great about it.

It would be difficult to find a better description of flow than this. The "best experiences" people have, the ones they feel most positive about, involve such moments of crisis where one is stretched beyond limits, where one is challenged to be creative—and, with any luck, succeeds. These moments of deep flow are the manifestation of what I have described as "soul," that is, of a person's being transformed through his or her efforts into someone more complex than he had been before.

As we have seen in previous chapters, when the conditions of flow are present, the experience includes a focusing of attention on a limited task; a forgetting of personal problems and of the self; a sense of control; and obliviousness to time. These are the elements of the inner state of consciousness that make whatever we are doing worth doing for its own sake. If management can provide an environment in which such experiences can flourish, the organization will run efficiently, and the staff will recognize that instead of stifling them, the job supports their growth.

If flow is absent, work turns into drudgery, and the worker loses his or her creative initiative. As William Stavropoulos says: "I think that you have to do what you like, so when you get up in the morning you say: 'Hey, I'm looking forward to this! I have some tough things to do. But I'm looking forward to it, because I like it.'" Douglas Yearley agrees with this assessment: "The first thing I say is enjoy what you're doing, because if you don't enjoy it, it's tedium and then you go off and do something else. Always maintain a sense of humor and balance outside of work, so that you don't become so engaged that you lose perspective with what's going on around you. Work hard, be ethical, but most importantly, have fun. That's kind of trite, but I really feel it."

Entrepreneurs starting a new venture, and leaders of organizations involved in complex projects usually have many opportunities to experience flow in their work—unless the challenges become overwhelming, or alternatively, they become trivial and routine. Most of the leaders we interviewed literally can't wait to get to the job each morning. Christine Comaford Lynch's enthusiasm in describing her job is typical: "It's just like, 'Wow! This is fabulous!' It's just so neat to explore ideas and then to build stuff, and to interact with fascinating people. It's really fun also to make your investors happy. That's fun. Especially the people of the first fund who took a huge risk."

While executives may find many sources of flow in their work, what of the clerical workers, salespeople, service employees? The people who clean the offices, unload the trucks, answer irate customers on the phone all day? How much flow do they experience on the job? In many organizations, management believes that question is not relevant, as it does not consider it the firm's responsibility to see to it that every employee has a job that is worth doing for its own sake, and in which one can grow in complexity. This "take it or leave it" attitude may work within the framework of a market model of human relations, but in all the ways we have discussed so far, it is simply not good business.

A Product That Helps Humankind

An organization with a powerful vision, one that provides flow and growth to its members, is by its very nature a wonderful creation. But there is still one more criterion to be met before such a firm can be said to be doing good business: namely, the nature of the work done by the organization. Is it a product or service that will make people happier in the long run, as well as in the present? Is it neutral with respect to human well-being? Or is it something that we will eventually regret was ever introduced? These are questions that resist simple answers, especially if one wishes to take into account the future consequences of present actions, which are often indeterminate.

Still, there are some obvious examples. Let's take one of the currently favorite targets of liberal critics—big tobacco. Given the accumulating evidence about the dangers of smoking, excruciating mental maneuvers must be necessary for people working in that industry to convince themselves that what they are doing is worthwhile. Fifty, or even as recently as twenty years ago one might have manufactured and sold cigarettes with a clear conscience, but it is becoming increasingly clear that despite the handsome profits it continues to provide, it is simply not a good business.

One might take the position that there is nothing inherently wrong with selling a product that is harmful, as long as people are aware of the danger and are willing to take their chances. But this "individual freedom" argument founders when applied to the young and to otherwise uninformed or inexperienced people. Making a dangerous product available may be legal, and it may even make sense from some perverse social Darwinist perspective that approves of the removal of the unfit, but it is hardly good business.

To move to a positive example, I recently met an engineer who works for a company that makes artificial lungs and other breathing apparatus to alleviate the suffering of patients with respiratory diseases. The firm was in a competitive market, the working hours were long and stressful, and the morale of the organization was suffering. Then the engineer had the idea of inviting some of the users of the firm's products to visit the plant, and describe the difference the machines had made in their lives. Strangely enough, up to that point the workers had not given much thought to the consequences of what they were doing. The machines they worked on provided immediate technical challenges and routine tasks, but their ultimate use was not often contemplated—they could just as well have been land mines or meat grinders. When families began to bring in their children who for the first time could breathe freely, relax, learn, and enjoy life because of the firm's product, it came as a revelation. The workers were energized by concrete evidence that their efforts really did improve people's lives, and the morale of the workplace was given a great lift.

Most issues that businesses deal with are not as clear-cut as the previous two examples. Consequences are typically more difficult to assess, and there might be honest differences in opinion regarding their nature. Many products that are beneficial at normal levels of use become harmful when overindulged. Whose responsibility is it, ultimately, when people make too much of a good thing? Let's take television, for example. It is now quite clear, as in the case with tobacco, that excessive television viewing is harmful to children. One might argue—as with guns or alcohol—that it should be the responsibility of parents, or the community, to see to it that such products are not abused, especially by children. Nevertheless, it is difficult to sustain the argument that providing means for stunting intellectual life is a good business.

Society will eventually have to come up with a formula that adds as a cost of operation the anticipated expenses that will be incurred from producing, selling, and using any given product. In small and isolated cases this is already being done, as in the example of a service station or car wash that is held responsible for cleaning up the chemical contamination it produces. But who will eventually bear the enormous costs of dealing with nuclear waste? Or with the addiction to mindless consumerism induced by advertising aimed at children? If humankind is to keep evolving, such questions must be addressed and answered soon.

In the meantime, one can start taking small steps in helping good business prevail within the existing market paradigm. Every worker should consider the outcome of what the organization does, not just in terms of its legality, but its likely long-term effects on human well-being. If after reflection unclouded by denial it turns out that the organization is likely to do more harm than good, one should try to improve on the outcome. If that is impossible, does it not make sense to look for a job that will satisfy one's conscience?

Another obvious way to support good business is by being more selective with one's investments. Many funds now offer "social choice" options, which invest in companies that have passed some level of environmental or political scrutiny. The threshold for qualifying is often very low, and may indicate nothing more than the fact that the firm is not involved in selling weapons to developing countries, or that it does not run sweatshops or kill baby seals.

But as consciousness about these issues keeps rising, enlightened investment policies can begin to exert a powerful counterforce to the prevailing single-minded logic of greed.

Finally, there are more direct economic and political venues for supporting good business. Firms like Patagonia, The Body Shop, Ben & Jerry's, L.L.Bean and Black Diamond make it part of their operating strategy to only use organic products, to take responsibility for the growth of their workers, to help foster an environmental ethic, and to devote a fraction of their earnings to causes that advance well-being.

Other firms and individuals use the profits of business to improve the quality of life by contributing enormous sums and great amounts of time to specific philanthropies devoted to health, education, the arts, culture, the prevention of delinquency, and so on. While these efforts are important for the enrichment of society, they depend more on the particular party's sense of responsibility than on the general conduct of business per se. In the past there have also been individual popes and noblemen who used their surplus wealth to build aqueducts, orphanages, and hospitals for the poor; who encouraged the arts and built lasting monuments while the institutions over which they presided kept society from advancing. The challenge for the future is to make the operation of business itself responsible for the improvement of life.

The Origin of the Principles of Good Business

A majority of the visionary leaders claim that the values by which they operate are so obvious and natural that there is no need to seek any explanation for them. Isn't is apparent that one should be honest, trusting, and concerned for the welfare of others? And in any case, they would argue, isn't honesty the best policy for running a profitable business? It would be wonderful if these principles were, in fact, so self-evident. But in reality they are not; as even our respondents recognize, many of their peers do not find them compelling. There are many successful, law-abiding business leaders who in private life are thoughtful and generous, but who do not regard taking responsibility for more than profits as part of their job.

We do not acquire values accidentally, or as the result of some divine dispensation. Nor do we make up values out of whole cloth. We have to learn them, as we learn the language our parents speak, or math, or making music. Values are memes, units of information passed down from one generation to another that shape our ways of thinking and our actions. The evolution of culture consists to a large extent in developing increasingly inclusive values. There is a tragic East African saying that goes: "Me and Somalia against the world, me and my tribe against Somalia, me and my family against my tribe, me and my brother against my family, me against my brother." The future depends on the opposite belief: "Me and everyone else for the universe."

The memes that point us in this direction have been traditionally preserved and transmitted by religions. Among the leaders we interviewed, the principles of good business were passed on through the belief systems of Judaism, Buddhism, Catholicism, various Protestant denominations, and the Mormon Church. To an extent entirely unexpected, faith in values acquired through a religious upbringing provided a solid platform for action to individuals involved in some of the most high-tech businesses, from aerospace to software.

It appears that despite the increasingly secular bent of our culture, religious traditions are still maintaining values that are essential for the evolution of culture and the improvement of human well-being. This is not to imply that it is necessarily the religions themselves that invented these values, or that the values are specifically rooted in religion. On the contrary, religions develop around some core values that people have discovered through trial and error as necessary for sustaining a good life. Our ancestors learned through experience that some behaviors are dangerous because they disrupt social harmony without improving individual well-being—like failing to respect parents and elders, having sex indiscriminately, or letting greed rule one's life. Yet they did not really understand the causes that made these things harmful. Religions evolved to make sense of why one should adopt certain values by creating a mythical framework in which those values were embedded. It is for this reason that so many of the core memes of the great religions are similar, while the narrative frameworks surrounding them are so varied.

Be that as it may, at this point good business depends to a large extent on the same values that undergird the major religious traditions. There are two specific ways that most people come to learn such values. The first path is taken by those leaders who adopt these principles by discovering their effectiveness through direct experience, or through a personal struggle with the ideas embedded in a variety of traditions. The second path is the more typical one: by following in the footsteps of one's parents. It is safe to say that it is enormously more efficient to take the hard-won learning "off the shelf," so to speak, than to have to reinvent it on one's own. Imagine the waste of psychic energy if each generation had to reinvent the wheel; it would be a loss of a similar magnitude if each generation had to discover for itself the particular values that make life worth living.

Yet the efficiency gained by adopting values that are tried and true has a potential negative aspect. Even the best religions, philosophies, and lifestyles have a way of losing their focus and original force over time. Sometimes they become the opposite of what they were intended to be: It is unlikely that Muhammad would recognize Islam as practiced by the Taliban, nor would Jesus Christ perceive his Gospel in the materialist message of many televangelists, or in the appeals of warring factions invoking his name in Ireland and elsewhere. Without the least trace of irony, the buckle of the Nazi storm troopers bore the legend: GOD IS WITH US. It is for this reason that getting to know oneself, as discussed in the previous chapter, must involve questioning which of the values one has learned are fundamental, and which are accidental historical accretions without real substance. To take the time for such questioning may ultimately undermine the efficiency provided by a ready-made belief system, but it is an effort worth investing in.

Whether couched in religious or secular language, the core principles of good business are learned early—in the family, the church, or in some other interpersonal setting like school, the Scouts, or an athletic team. To truly absorb these principles one has to be exposed to people who live by them, for they are most effectively passed on through example and interaction. In growing up with parents who love their work, who are honest and trusting, and who are rewarded with the respect of the community, a child will take for granted that theirs is the best way to live. Books are also useful, but they seldom do the job alone. Without good parents or other strong role models one can still become very successful, but it is unlikely that one will believe in the importance of striving for the common good.

And then there is the indispensable example of visionary leaders, like the ones we have met in this book, and the companies they represent. There are, of course, many other leaders and businesses whom we were unable to include in our study, but who are equally committed to creating a better world. Companies like Merck, Johnson & Johnson, Motorola, Hewlett-Packard, Sony, and Gallup shine like beacons guiding us through the roiling tides of greed toward the way to do good business. If more and more leaders of business would follow their lead—from small entrepreneurs to middle managers, to the captains of large industries—business would truly fulfill its potential to help make life happier for all.

Notes

Chapter 1: Leading the Future

page

4   **The Good Work in Business** project was started by three principal investigators: William Damon (Stanford University), Mihaly Csikszentmihalyi (Claremont Graduate University), and Howard Gardner (Harvard University). It was supported by grant number 629 of the Templeton Foundation. In the fall of 1998, fourteen individuals with extensive experience in business (mainly CEOs and professors at leading business schools) were asked to: "identify business leaders who combine high achievement with strong moral commitment." "Moral commitment" was defined as "long-term dedication to goals that advance the interests of the community, the people living in it, and humanity in general." A total of more than 140 business leaders were nominated. Out of this total we selected two dozen who had been identified by three or more of the nominators as meeting our criteria. Of these, eighteen agreed to be interviewed with a structured interview protocol that usually took two hours to complete, and was focused on the following topics: respondents' goals and purposes; beliefs and values; work processes; formative background; community and family; and so on.

In addition to the interviews, extensive biographical and other written material on each respondent were consulted.

Using the same protocol, we interviewed twenty-one additional leaders whose reputation suggested we should include them in the study. These thirty-nine individuals are the ones I will refer to in these pages as *visionary leaders.*

Interviews were conducted by the three principal investigators and their staff. At Stanford University this consisted of Barbara Tolentino (Stanford project team leader), Mollie Galloway, Aasha Joshi, Ben Kirshner, Kristen Palmer, Liza Percer, Susan Verducci, and Joel Zarrow. At Harvard University the team was Kim Barberich (Harvard project team leader), Lynn Barendson, Jonathon Heller, Mimi Michaelson, Dan Dillon, and Marcy LeLacheur. The Claremont Graduate University team consisted of Jeanne Nakamura (Claremont project team leader), Heather Campbell, David Creswell, Jeremy Hunter, and Martha Uenishi.

Of the thirty-nine respondents, thirty-three were male. Ages ranged from less than fifty years (N = 6) to more than sixty-five (N = 11). Business sectors represented were computer software and hardware (5); manufacturing (4); retail (5); biotechnology (4); entertainment (3); real estate (3); venture capital (2); management consulting (2); petroleum industry (2); aerospace (2); and one each from mining, restaurant franchising, financial investment, education, product design, services, and transportation.

Interviews were obtained from the following persons:

Norman Augustine (former CEO, Lockheed Martin)
Deborah Besemer (CEO, BrassRing Systems)
Peter Bijur (CEO, Texaco)
Yvon Chouinard (founder, Patagonia)
Christine Comaford Lynch (managing director, Artemis Ventures)
James Davis (founder and CEO, New Balance)
Max DePree (former CEO, chairman, Herman Miller)
Kenneth Derr (chairman and CEO, Chevron)
Richard DeVos (cofounder and CEO, Amway)
Aaron Feuerstein (CEO, Malden Mills)
Jane Fonda
Orit Gadiesh (CEO, Bain & Co.)
Leon Gorman (chairman, L.L.Bean)
Jack Greenberg (chairman and CEO, McDonald's)
Gerald Greenwald (former chairman and CEO, United Airlines)
Michael Hackworth (chairman, Cirrus Logic)
Richard Jacobsen (partner, WSJ Properties)
David Kelley (founder and chairman, IDEO)

Lars Kolind (former CEO, Oticon)
John Leonis (CEO, Litton Industries)
Byron Lewis, Sr. (founder and CEO, UniWorld Group)
Michael Markkula (cofounder, Apple Computer)
J. Irwin Miller (honorary chairman, CEO, Cummins)
Michael Murray (former VP, Microsoft)
Mads Ovlisen (CEO, Novo Nordisk)
C. William Pollard (chairman, ServiceMaster)
Anita Roddick (founder, The Body Shop)
T. J. Rodgers (president and CEO, Cypress Semiconductor
    Corporation)
Timothy Rowe (founder and CEO, Cambridge Incubator)
Robert Shapiro (former chairman and CEO, Monsanto)
John Sobrato (founder and chairman, Sobrato Development
    Companies)
John Sperling (founder, University of Phoenix)
William Stavropoulos (president and CEO, Dow Chemical)
Sir John Templeton (Financial Investment)
Ted Turner (vice chairman, AOL Time Warner)
McDonald Williams (chairman emeritus, Trammell Crow)
Ann Winblad (cofounder and partner, Hummer Winblad Venture
    Partners)
Douglas Yearley (former CEO, Phelps Dodge)
Alfred Zeien (former CEO, Gillette)

The transcript of these interviews provides the bulk of the quotes used in this volume to illustrate how visionary leaders operate and how they see the world.

7   **Sustained indefinitely.** The critique of materialist society and the economy that sustains it is so vast and generally well known that repeating it here seems unnecessary. For an introduction to these topics, see for instance, *Foundation for the Future* (2000).

10   **Karl Marx.** A recent analysis by Stiglitz (2002) suggests that the widening chasm between rich and poor countries repeats on a global scale the conflict between social classes within nations that caused so much misery in the past century. See also Soros (2001).

12   **Randone.** Interviews with Enrico Randone and [Elisabeth Noelle-Neumann] were conducted for my book on creativity (Csikszentmihalyi, 1996).

15   For the fascinating history of **Cummins** Engines, see Cruikshank and Sicilia (1997).

17   In 1939 the Austrian economist Joseph **Schumpeter** developed the notion of recurring business cycles that are accelerated when old firms, instead of evolving, go out of business. (See Schumpeter (1985).

Chapter 2: The Business of Happiness

page

21   The way **Aristotle** understood happiness (for example, in *Nichomachean Ethics*, Book 1, and at the end of Book 9) is still extremely useful. For some recent commentaries on how Aristotle's views fare in light of contemporary thought one might turn to MacIntyre (1984) or Robinson (1976).

22   **After almost a century . . . psychologists have become interested in studying happiness,** even if they don't always call it that. "Subjective well-being" or "hedonic psychology" are some of the favorite synonyms with a more scientific sound (Kahneman, Diener, and Schwarz, 1999). Even a new scholarly journal dedicated to the topic has recently started publication, the *Journal of Happiness Studies*.

22   Psychologists who believe that **genes have a great role** in determining happiness include Lykken (1999) and Buss (2000). The exact amount of genetic contribution is still heavily debated, with the battle lines drawn at about the fiftieth percentile. In other words, it is generally accepted that about half of a person's score on happiness surveys is a result of genetic predisposition.

22   A good **summary of happiness research,** accessible although becoming somewhat dated in this rapidly growing field of research, is the one by Myers (1993); see also his more recent statement in Myers (2000). The comparisons of happiness in different nations were pioneered by Inglehart (1990); see also Veenhoven (1992) and Diener (2000).

22   The **effects of political conditions** in South Africa on the happiness of the inhabitants is reported in Møller (2001). A special issue of the *Journal of Happiness Studies* (including Veenhoven, 2001) is dedicated to finding out how economic, political, and social changes in Russia have impacted on happiness. In general, happiness is affected more by social comparisons than by income or purchasing ability. What makes people unhappy is not so much the lack of money, but the gap

between themselves and more affluent people who don't seem to deserve their wealth (Schyns, 2001; see also Lyubomirski and Ross, 1997).

23   Some of the seminal work of **Abraham Maslow,** which had a large influence on psychology, includes Maslow (1968, 1971). His contribution to business management was based on his awkwardly titled book, *Eupsychian Management* (1962—retitled *Maslow on Management* in 1995), and on the further development of his thought by management experts like Peter Drucker (1999).

24   Some of the most eloquent arguments for **self-actualization** can be found in the work of the psychologist-turned-statesman John Gardner (1990), who has been a firm believer in the human ability to live at 100 percent of its potential.

25   **Dante Alighieri** is considered one of the greatest poets who ever lived, but some of his keenest insights into human psychology appear in his lesser-known political tracts, such as *De Monarchia*, from which I translated the passage in the text.

25   A **happy organization.** That business needs a new paradigm, based on the inspired commitment of the workforce (what I would call intrinsic motivation) has been widely recognized lately—at least in theory. See for instance, Ellsworth (2002), Scott (2000), Thomas (2000), and Weihrouch (2000).

26   **John Locke.** In his *Essays* (1689), Book 2, Chapter 21, page 63.

26   Loyall Rue (1994) provides an extensive review of the role of **deceit** in evolution.

27   The advantages of **"creative destruction"** in economics were first hailed by the Austrian economist Joseph Schumpeter (1939). For a contemporary application of these ideas, see Foster and Kaplan (2001).

28   **Materialism.** Recent studies collected in Schmuck and Sheldon (2001) show that well-being is enhanced when we devote energy to goals that reach beyond the momentary and the selfish. We feel happier pursuing short-term goals than no goals at all; when pursuing long-term goals rather than short-term goals; when working to better ourselves rather than just having pleasure; and we feel happier when working for the well-being of another person, group, or larger entity as opposed to just investing effort in self-centered goals.

29   The notion of **psychological complexity** based on differentiation and integration is developed in Csikszentmihalyi (1993); see also Inghilleri (1999).

30   There is considerable argument about the amount of **stress** workers

experience nowadays—or more precisely, about how much of the stress is self-inflicted. For a great proportion of families living at the edge of subsistence the need for both parents (or for a single mother) to work at more than one job is a necessity (see Ehrenreich, 2001); but for many others excessive work is caused by indoctrination into a consumer lifestyle.

30   That **evolution** depends on the unfolding of material complexity has been argued by many others including the biologist Ernst Mayr (1982), the paleontologist Teilhard de Chardin (1965), and by theoreticians of the newly emerging science of complexity (for example, Waldrop, 1992).

32   That the **life cycle** consists of dialectical swings between differentiation and integration leading to complexity is implicit in the developmental models of Erikson (1950), Kegan (1982), Levinson (1980), Loevinger (1976), and Vaillant (2001), among others.

35   Since the interview, **Jane Fonda** did join a traditional faith-based religious community.

Chapter 3: Happiness in Action

page
38   **The experience of flow** was first described in Csikszentmihalyi (1975). Later studies are reported in Csikszentmihalyi 1990, 1997, Csikszentmihalyi and Csikszentmihalyi, 1988. The citations from rock climbers, surgeons, dancers, and so on, come from these sources unless otherwise indicated.

40   The quote of the **mother** describing flow while reading to her daughter is from Allison and Duncan (1988).

45   Flow in sailing is described by Pardey and Pardey (1982); see also Macbeth (1988).

46   **Solitary confinement.** The importance of being able to experience flow even under the harshest conditions is discussed by Logan (1988) and in Csikszentmihalyi (1990, Chapter 9).

46   How some young people grow up thinking **"there is nothing to do"** in their environment is described in Csikszentmihalyi and Schneider (2000); see also Hunter (2001).

47   The **bicycle racer**'s quote is from Jackson and Csikszentmihalyi (1999). The ones from **poets and writers** are from a study by Susan Perry (1999) who interviewed some of the foremost U.S. authors to

determine what obstacles they encounter to experiencing flow in their work, and how they overcome them.

51 **Olympic runner's** quote is from Jackson and Csikszentmihalyi (1999). Susan Jackson, a sports psychologist teaching in Australia, has collected a large number of interviews with elite athletes around the world, as well as conducting many questionnaire-based studies of flow in sports.

54 The **Bailey** quote is from Jackson and Csikszentmihalyi (1999), the one from **Davison** is from Perry (1999), and the one from the climber **Doug Robinson** is from Robinson (1969, p. 6).

55 The quote from **Dennis Eberl** is in Eberl (1969, p.13). Rock climbing is a quintessential flow activity that provides no financial and very little status rewards, yet can often result in the loss of life. For those who are interested in reading further about the strange joys of climbing, there is an excellent description by the Italian climber and poet Guido Rey in his *Peaks and Precipices* of 1914 or in the more recent books by Knight (1970) and Lukan (1968). The recent commercialization of climbing and the new dangers attendant to guided expeditions to the highest summits is described in Krakauer (1997).

56 The relationship between **self-esteem** and flow was studied by Ann Wells (1988).

56 The psychiatrist **Viktor Frankl,** who barely survived the Nazi concentration camps, left a wonderful account of how focusing on what's meaningful in life can keep a person sane even under the worst circumstances (1963).

59 The quote from **Tolstoy** is in the new revised translation by Constance Garnett (1993).

60 For the connection between **flow and religion** see for example, Eno (1990) who describes the origins of Confucianism as rooted in flow-like ritual; Massimini and Delle Fave (1991), and Inghilleri (1999). The quote **"It's not God . . ."** is in Perry (1999, p. 74).

60 The data on **religiosity** in Western nations is from Marniga (2001).

Chapter 4: Flow and Growth

page

69 **Teenagers who are in flow.** The importance of experiencing flow in productive activities has been shown by various studies including Csikszentmihalyi, Rathunde, and Whalen (1993) and Hunter (2001).

69   The concept of **social capital** was developed by the French sociologist Pierre Bourdieu (1977, 1993), and the American sociologist James Coleman (1988, 1990).

70   **Ibuka's mission statement** is quoted in Collins and Porras (1997, p. 50).

71   The **experience sampling method** is described in articles and books that use this approach to research; for instance Csikszentmihalyi and Csikszentmihalyi (1988); Kubey and Csikszentmihalyi (1990); Csikszentmihalyi and Schneider (2000).

75   **Frequency of flow.** The U.S. survey was conducted by the Gallup Organization in 1998; the one in Germany by the Allensbach Institute (Noelle-Neumann, 1995).

76   The first empirical investigation of **psychological capital** has started in our laboratory (Hunter, 2001).

76   Drucker's definition of **capital** reads: "capital (that is, the resources witheld from current consumption and allocated instead to future expectations)" (1985, p. 27).

76   The great American psychologist of the nineteenth century, William James, was the first to spell out the importance of **attention** in the psychic economy (1890, especially Volume 1, Chapter 11). Since that time many have written on the topic, but it is fair to say that we still have only the most superficial understanding of how attentional processes are formed and how they determine our lives (Csikszentmihalyi 1978, Kahneman 1973).

78   For the **limits of attention** in speech and hearing, see Nusbaum and Schwab (1986) and in general Csikszentmihalyi (1997).

79   James Coleman (1988) identified the network of relationships a person can draw on as **social capital.** For instance, having a father who went to Harvard is social capital for his children who may have a better chance to be admitted as a consequence. A similar concept, **cultural capital,** refers to the knowledge a person has the opportunity to absorb by growing up in a given environment. For instance, we find that teenagers whose homes contain more than fifty books have a better chance of getting admitted to elite colleges, while children who have a TV set in their bedrooms have a much slighter chance—controlling for parental education, income, and so on (preliminary results from the Sloan Study, see Csikszentmihalyi and Schneider, 2000).

79   **Postponement of gratification.** The paradoxical finding about workers enjoying their job, yet wanting to be elsewhere was first signaled in

Csikszentmihalyi and LeFevre (1989). Similar results are reported by Abdumedeh (2002).

80   **Asian American teens.** See Asakawa and Csikszentmihalyi, 2000.

Chapter 5: Why Flow Doesn't Happen on the Job

page

85   **People are built to work.** Many studies show that unemployed persons suffer psychologically as well as economically. For instance, based on comparative studies of almost 170,000 respondents in sixteen nations, Ronald Inglehart (1990) concluded that while 83 percent of white-collar and 77 percent of blue-collar workers said they were "satisfied with life," only 61 percent of the unemployed did. One should note that such a difference does not necessarily imply that lack of work makes one dissatisfied. Perhaps people dissatisfied with life have less of an incentive to find a job, or perhaps individuals who are physically ill are both less satisfied and less likely to work. However, other studies (e.g. Haworth and Ducker, 1991) suggest that people become less satisfied after they lose a job, in part because the range of experiences they can have gets impoverished as a result.

87   **Young people's career expectations.** In a study of more than four thousand U.S. teenagers (Csikszentmihalyi and Schneider, 2000, p. 45), the job that most of them expect to have is that of doctor (10 percent), followed by businessperson (7 percent), lawyer (7 percent), teacher (7 percent), athlete (6 percent) and actor (5 percent). These six jobs account for the expectations of almost half the sample. Although a few listed "pimp" and "drug dealer," very few young persons looked forward to traditional industrial or craft occupations—let alone blue-collar jobs. Regardless of economic background, the majority of high school students expects to have professional jobs after it graduates, and to earn around a quarter million dollars a year. The 7 percent of students who expect to be **teachers** stand out from the rest by having much more modest and realistic earning expectations.

88   The **estimate of time worked in traditional hunting-gathering societies** is from the anthropologist Marshall Sahlins (1972).

88   For the **conditions of work in traditional societies** see for example, Massimini and Delle Fave (1988) and Inghilleri (1999).

89   **Australian aborigines.** How a kangaroo was divided in former times at

Alice Springs is described in Firth (1958, p. 71). Firth also reports similar ways of spreading the wealth in other traditional societies such as Melanesia, Burma, and Samoa.

89   **John Hope Franklin's** attitude to work is described in Csikszentmihalyi (1996, p. 207). **George Klein** mentions the flow he experiences from his work in *The Atheist and the Holy City* (1990, p. 154).

93   **Skills . . . matched to the opportunities.** One cause of depression and coronary disease is to have a job with high demands and low decision latitude (corresponding to the anxiety condition in the flow model— that is, high challenges, low skills); see Karasek et al. (1981).

95   **Division of labor.** The semiofficial *DOT*, or *Dictionary of Occupational Titles* published by the U.S. Department of Labor, lists thousands of occupations, including such esoteric ones as "blind hooker," "cookie breaker," "dice spotter," "finger waver," "hand shaker," "religious ritual slaughterer," and "worm-bed attendant." (*Harper's*, August 2000, p. 31). Similar fine lines of specialization exist now among knowledge workers, as the want ads of any newspaper will show. A single issue of the *Chronicle of Higher Education* (July 7, 2000), listed among hundreds of job openings those for "information literacy minority residency," "production operations or information systems," "national outreach manager," "director of Web services," "regulatory compliance manager," "director of disability services," and "director of major gifts." One conclusion that might be drawn from this admittedly small sample is that jobs for knowledge workers have long titles.

96   A good review of research findings about **stress at work** can be found in Zuzanek (2000); for an impressionistic but vivid account see Ehrenreich (2001).

98   Why **different jobs are attractive** to young people is described in Csikszentmihalyi and Schneider (2000, p. 49).

99   **"Work" is unpleasant.** By sixth grade, whenever American children label something they do as "work," they also see it as something sad and boring (although important); whereas when they label something as "play" they see it as happy and enjoyable, but unimportant (Csikszentmihalyi and Schneider, 2000, p. 73).

100   **"Good work."** What doing good work in various occupations means, and what the major obstacles to it are, have been dealt with in a recent study by Gardner, Csikszentmihalyi, and Damon (2001).

100   **Postmodern business.** See for instance the debate between Collins and Porras (1994) who argue for the value of stable business organizations,

and Foster and Kaplan (2001) who take the postmodern deconstructionist position arguing that long-lived companies are less profitable than the median for the SP500. The latter position is an elaboration of the one advocated earlier last century by the Austrian economist Joseph Schumpeter (1939), who coined the term "creative destruction." An excellent analysis of this debate is in Ellsworth (2002).

100   **Impermanent work environments.** By the early 1990s, only 55 percent of full- and part-time employees in the United States worked a "traditional" workweek. This and other "flextime" patterns are reviewed in Zuzanek (2000). Epstein et al. (1998) discuss the obstacles to advancement for those who do not work a traditional workweek. The psychological stresses caused by time pressure have been amply documented; for reviews see Rifkin (1987), Robinson and Godbey (1997), and Zuzanek (2000). Despite stupendous technological advances that were going to make life more comfortable and leisurely, people in industrial societies feel more pressed for time than they have in the past. In the United States more men and women reported feeling "always rushed" in 1985 than in 1975 and 1965 (Robinson, 1993). In 1977 40 percent of Americans stated that they "never have enough time" to get things finished on the job; by 1997 the proportion had risen to 60 percent (Bondl, Galinsky and Swanberg, 1997).

101   **The distinction between a job, a career, and a calling (or vocation).** Some recent empirical studies of workers who hold these attitudes (distinctions originally proposed by Robert Bellah) have been conducted by Wrzesniewski and Dutton. For instance, hospital cleaners who see their job as a *calling* describe their work as critical to healing patients by brightening their days and enhancing their well-being. Hospital cleaners who see their work as a *job* describe it as simply cleaning up rooms. (Wrzesniewski and Dutton, 2001).

102   The reference is to Johann Wolfgang von **Goethe,** *Faust,* Act II: *"Zum Sehen geboren, Zum Schauen bestellt"*—and it is the way Peter Drucker describes his attitude toward his life work.

106   **Changes in values.** From the annual surveys of more than 200,000 U.S. students entering college (for a total of approximately 6.5 million). Data are from Dey, Astin, and Korn (1991) and subsequent annual reports (Sax et al. 1998).

Chapter 6: Building Flow in Organizations

page

107   **Building an organization.** (Collins and Porras, 1994). In his more recent book, Jim Collins (2001) makes the point that "great" companies
start with hiring the right people even before they have developed a
corporate strategy.

108   **Stupendous work in dismal surroundings.** Warren Bennis (1997) gives
excellent examples of how groups involved in cutting-edge projects
can maintain morale even under miserable conditions.

113   **Study of outstanding colleges.** Funded by the Hewlett Foundation, and directed by Howard Gardner, Bill Damon, and Mihaly
Csikszentmihalyi.

118   **Donald Campbell** was one of the most creative psychologists of the last
century; see for instance Campbell (1965).

123–   **John Reed** and **Enrico Randone** referred to on the next page were
124   some of the individuals interviewed for my book *Creativity* (Csikszentmihalyi, 1996).

131   **Determine your strengths.** Two of the more committed writers on this
topic are Don Clifton (Buckingham & Clifton, 2000), who for many
years led the Gallup Organization according to this principle, and
Martin Seligman (2002), a very influential psychologist and former
president of the American Psychological Association.

135   **Matteo Ricci** (1552–1610) was an Italian Jesuit who, despite great initial skepticism, was able to convince Chinese intellectuals that the
West was not entirely barbarian.

138   **Work nonstandard hours.** Some of the problems workers encounter
when they work on flextime and at home were discussed a decade ago
by Pressner (1989) and recently by Zuzanek (2000). If working at
home is to be a boon rather than a bane, it is important for the worker
to develop a personal discipline to structure the workday, otherwise
anxiety will increase and productivity drop. Of course the savings on
commuting time alone can be enormous, and thus justify lower productivity per unit of time.

Chapter 7: The Soul of Business

page

143   **C. William Pollard** has written insightfully on the issue of soul in business organizations. The quote continues: "When there is alignment between the cause of the firm and the cause of its people, move over— because there will be extraordinary performance." (1996, p. 45)

144   **Organization of matter.** The French paleontologist and Jesuit Teilhard de Chardin (1965) proposed that organized matter always disposes of some extra "radial energy" which could be used to raise its own level of complexity. In the human brain, that energy is soul. Teilhard's ideas were met with ridicule and skepticism by the scientific community fifty years ago, but his claims no longer seem so outrageous in light of current understanding.

145   **Care at the core of the soul.** Most religions and philosophies teach that investing one's energies for the sake of others is the highest manifestation of human nature, or soul. Charity is one of the cardinal virtues of Christianity, and its analog is prominent in Buddhism, Judaism, Hinduism, and Islam. Among recent philosophers this is the conclusion reached by Martin Heidegger (1962). See also the important study by the psychologists Ann Colby and William Damon (1992), *Some Do Care.*

147   **Vision.** Another word that overlaps considerably with vision is the concept of *purpose.* The importance of purpose in leadership has been well described recently by Ellsworth (2002).

151   **Religious faith.** It has lately become again admissible to talk seriously about religious faith in connection with leadership in business; see for instance Banks and Powell (2000).

154   **Values exploited.** As mentioned earlier, Rue (1994) gives a superb review of the role of deception in survival and evolution. Pretending to be what one is not so as to take advantage of others is a frequent strategy that one must always be wary of.

156   The scholar who more than anyone else has brought **optimism** under scientific scrutiny is Martin Seligman (2002). He has shown, for instance, that political leaders who use more optimistic rhetoric in their speeches tend to get elected over candidates whose message is less optimistic (Zullow and Seligman, 1990). A somewhat similar approach is the one taken by Howard Gardner, a cognitive psychologist who sees leadership as depending largely on the kind of narratives leaders present to their audiences (Gardner, 1995).

Chapter 8: Creating Flow in Life

page

167 The kinds of **self-deception** all of us are vulnerable to, and their origins, is discussed in Chapter 3 of *The Evolving Self* (Csikszentmihalyi, 1993).

169 **Traditional religious . . . values.** The social sciences have not been kind to religion, pointing out the many inconsistencies and improbabilities that religious beliefs entail. Recently, however, religion has received support from an improbable source: evolutionary theory. David Sloan Wilson (2002), for instance, points out that from an evolutionary perspective survival trumps truth or logic. In human evolution, groups that are able to cooperate fare better than those that are riven by conflict and dissension. This sort of inner harmony has been best achieved—at least so far—by a binding religion. Thus religion is an adaptation that enhances group survival, which in turn facilitates the survival of individuals. Most of the visionary leaders would not disagree with this conclusion.

169 **Leadership is a function of questions.** That creativity depends in large part on the ability to ask the right questions was something Jacob W. Getzels brought to the attention of psychologists (Getzels and Csikszentmihalyi 1976). The notion that problem *finding* rather than problem *solving* is crucial to creativity was applied later by Silver (1985) to the practice of entrepreneurship. See also Runco (1994).

171 **John Gardner**'s career is described in Csikszentmihalyi (1996).

176 **Out of control CEOs.** John R. O'Neil, who has consulted and counseled many business leaders, describes the traps of successful executives in an excellent book subtitled *When Winning at Work Means Losing at Life* (1993).

177 Warren Bennis discusses **"management of the self"** in his aptly titled book, *Managing People Is Like Herding Cats.* (1997, p. 86).

179 The way **Linus Pauling** worked is described in Csikszentmihalyi (1996, p. 118)

Chapter 9: The Future of Business

page
189   The financial pressures on **newspaper**s and the consequent difficulty of doing exhaustive reporting in the media are detailed in Gardner, Csikszentmihalyi, and Damon (2001).

205   **Dangers of smoking.** Besides the mounting epidemiological evidence, some of the more startling findings are those coming from the Harvard Study of Aging, one of the most careful and extensive longitudinal investigations in the world, recently described by George Vaillant. For example, while 64 percent of men who drank little and smoked little had no physical disabilities at ages seventy-five to eighty, only 24 percent of those who drank little but were heavy smokers were still hale and hearty at that age (Vaillant, 2002, p. 208).

207   **Excessive television viewing** for children. See for instance the review in Kubey and Csikszentmihalyi (2002).

References

Alighieri, Dante (1317). *De Monarchia,* Florence: Rostagno, 1921. Book 1. Chapter 13.

Allison, M. T. and M. C. Duncan. *Optimal Experience: Psychological Studies of Flow in Consciousness,* M. Csikszentmihalyi and I. S. Csikszentmihalyi. New York: Cambridge University Press, 1988, pp. 118-137.

Asakawa, K. and M. Csikszentmihalyi. "Feelings of Connectedness and Internalization of Values in Asian American Adolescents." *Journal of Youth and Adolescence,* 29 (2000) pp. 121–45.

Banks, R. and K. Powell. (eds.) *Faith in Leadership: How Leaders Live Out Their Faith in Their Work—and Why It Matters.* San Francisco: Jossey-Bass, 2000.

Bellah, R.N., R. Madsen, et al., *Habits of the Heart: Individualism and Commitment in American Life.* New York: Harper, 1986.

Bennis, W. *Managing People Is Like Herding Cats.* Provo, Utah: Executive Excellence Publishing, 1997.

———. and P. Biederman. *Organizing Genius: The Secrets of Creative Collaboration.* Reading, Mass: Addison-Wesley, 1997.

Bondl, J. T., E. Galinsky, and J. E. Swanberg. *The 1997 National Study of the Changing Workforce.* New York: Families and Work Institute, 1997.

Bourdieu, P. *Outline of a Theory of Practice,* tr. R. Nice. Cambridge, UK: Cambridge University Press, 1977.

———. *The Field of Cultural Production.* New York: Columbia University Press, 1993.

Buckingham, M. and D. Clifton. *Now, Discover Your Strengths.* New York: Simon & Schuster, 2000.

Buss, D. M. "The Evolution of Happiness." *American Psychologist,* 55: 1 (2000), pp. 15–24.

Campbell, D. "Variation and selective retention in socio-cultural evolution." In eds. H. R. Barringer, G. I. Blankston, and R. W. Monks. *Social Change in Developing Areas.* Cambridge, Mass.: Schenkman, 1965.

Colby, A. and W. Damon. *Some Do Care: Contemporary Lives of Moral Commitment.* New York: The Free Press, 1992.

Coleman, J. S. "Social Capital in the Creation of Human Capital." *American Journal of Sociology*, 94, (1988), pp. 95–120.

———. *Foundations of Social Theory.* Cambridge, Mass.: Belknap Press, 1990.

Collins, J. C. *Good to Great.* New York: HarperBusiness, 2001.

———. and J. I. Porras. *Built to Last: Successful Habits of Visionary Companies.* New York: HarperBusiness, 1994.

Cruikshank, J. L. and D. B. Sicilia, *The Engine That Could: Seventy-Five Years of Values-Driven Change at Cummins Engine Company.* Boston: Harvard Business School Press, 1997.

Csikszentmihalyi, M. *Beyond Boredom and Anxiety.* San Francisco: Jossey Bass, 1975.

———. "Attention and the Wholistic Approach to Behavior." In *The Stream of Consciousness*, eds. K. S. Pope and J. L. Singer. New York: Plenum, 1978, pp. 335–58.

———. *Flow: The Psychology of Optimal Experience.* New York: HarperCollins, 1990.

———. *The Evolving Self: A Psychology for the Third Millennium.* New York: HarperCollins, 1993.

———. *Creativity: Flow and the Psychology of Discovery and Invention.* New York: HarperCollins, 1996.

———. *Finding Flow:* The Psychology of Engagement with Everyday Life. New York: Basic Books, 1997.

———. and I. S. Csikszentmihalyi. eds. *Optimal Experience: Psychological Studies of Flow in Consciousness.* New York: Cambridge University Press, 1988.

———. and J. LeFevre. "Optimal Experience in Work and Leisure." *Journal of Personality and Social Psychology* 56:5, (1989), pp. 815–22.

———, K. Rathunde, and S. Whalen. *Talented Teenagers: The Roots of Success and Failure.* New York: Cambridge University Press, 1993.

———. and B. Schneider. *Becoming Adult: How Teenagers Prepare for the World of Work.* New York: Basic Books, 2000.

Dey, E. L., A. W. Astin, and W. S. Korn. *The American Freshman: Twenty-Five Year Trends, 1966–1990.* Los Angeles: Higher Education Research Institute, 1991.

Diener, E. "Subjective Well-being: The Science of Happiness and a Proposal for a National Index." *American Psychologist*, 55:1, (2001), pp. 34–43.

Drucker, P. F. *Innovation and Entrepreneurship: Practice and Principles*. New York: HarperBusiness, 1985.

————. *Management Challenges for the 21ˢᵗ Century*. New York: HarperBusiness, 1999.

Eberl, D. "Matterhorn." *Ascent*, 9 (1969), pp. 11–15.

Ehrenreich, B. *Nickel and Dimed to Death*. New York: Metropolitan Books, 2001.

Ellsworth, R. *Leading with Purpose: The New Corporate Realities*. Stanford, Calif.: Stanford University Press, 2002.

Eno, R. *The Confucian Creation of Heaven*. New York: SUNY Press, 1990.

Epstein, C. F., C. Seron, B. Oglensky, and R. Saute. *The Part-time Paradox: Time Norms, Professional Life, and Gender*. New York: Routledge, 1998.

Erikson, E. *Childhood and Society*. New York: Norton, 1950.

Firth, R. *Human Types, an Introduction to Social Anthropology*. New York: New American Library, 1958.

Foster, R. and S. Kaplan. *Creative Destruction: Why Companies That Are Built to Last Underperform the Market—and How to Successfully Transform Them*. New York: Doubleday, 2001.

Foundation for the Future (2000) *Humanity 3000*. Bellevue, Wash.: Foundation for the Future, 2000.

Frankl, V. *Man's Search for Meaning*. New York: Washington Square Press, 1963.

Gardner, J. *On Leadership*. New York: The Free Press, 1990.

Gardner, H. *Leading Minds: an Anatomy of Leadership*. New York: Basic Books, 1995.

————, M. Csikszentmihalyi, and W. Damon. *Good Work: When Excellence and Ethics Meet*. New York: Basic Books, 2001.

Getzels, J. W. and M. Csikszentmihalyi. *The Creative Vision: A Longitudinal Study of Artists*. New York: Wiley, 1976.

Haworth, J. T. and J. Ducker. Psychological Well-Being and Access to Categories of Experience in Unemployed Young Adults." *Leisure Studies* 10 (1991), pp. 265–74.

Heidegger, M. *Being and Time*. Trans. J. Macquarrie and E. Robinson. New York: SCM Press, 1962.

Hunter, J. "Vital Powers and Wasted Possibilities: Engaged and Bored Teenagers in America." Unpub. Doctoral Dissert. Chicago: The University of Chicago, 2001.

Inghilleri, P. *From Subjective Experience to Cultural Change*. New York: Cambridge University Press, 1999.

Inglehart, R. *Culture Shift in Advanced Industrial Society*. Princeton, NJ: Princeton University Press, 1990.

232   References

"Inside McKinsey." *Business Week,* July 8, 2002.

Jackson, S. A. and M. Csikszentmihalyi. *Flow in Sports.* Urbana, Ill.: Human Kinetics, 1999.

James, W. *Principles of Psychology.* New York: Henry Holt, 1890.

Kahneman, D. *Attention and Effort.* Englewood Cliffs, NJ: Prentice-Hall, 1973.

————, E. Diener, and N. Schwarz. *Well-Being: The Foundations of Hedonistic Psychology.* New York: Russell Sage Foundation, 1999.

Karasek, R., D. Baker, F. Marxer, A. Ahlbom, and T. Theorell. "Job Description Latitude, Job Demand, and Cardiovascular Disease: A Prospective Study of Swedish Men." *American Journal of Public Health,* 71 (1981), pp. 694–705.

Kegan, R. *The Evolving Self: Problem and Process in Human Development.* Cambridge, Mass.: Harvard University Press, 1982.

Klein, G. *The Atheist and the Holy City: Encounters and Reflections.* Cambridge, Mass.: The MIT Press, 1990.

Knight, M. *Return to the Alps.* New York: Friends of the Earth, 1970.

Krakauer, J. *Into Thin Air.* New York: Villard Books, 1997.

Kubey, R. and M. Csikszentmihalyi. *Television and the Quality of Life: How Viewing Shapes Everyday Experience.* Hillsdale, NJ: Erlbaum, 1990.

———— and M. Csikszentmihalyi. "Television Addiction: Not Just a Metaphor." *Scientific American,* 286, 2, (2002) 74–81.

Levinson, D. J. "Toward a Conception of the Adult Life Course. In *Themes of Work and Love in Adulthood,* eds. N. Smelser and E. Erikson. Cambridge, Mass: Harvard University Press, 1980, pp. 265–290.

Logan, R. D. In *Optimal Experience: Psychological Studies of Flow in Consciousness,* eds. M. Csikszentmihalyi and I. S. Csikszentmihalyi. New York: Cambridge University Press, 1988, pp. 172–82.

Locke, J. *An Essay Concerning Human Understanding.* Oxford: Oxford University Press, 1689, p. 63.

Loevinger, J. *Ego Development.* San Francisco: Jossey-Bass, 1976.

Lukan, K., ed. *The Alps and Alpinism.* New York: Coward-McCann, 1968.

Lykken, D. *Happiness.* New York: Golden Books, 1999.

Lyubomirski, S. and L. Ross. "Hedonic Consequences of Social Comparisons: A Contrast of Happy and Unhappy People." *Journal of Personality and Social Psychology,* 73 (1997), pp. 1141–57.

Macbeth, J. "Ocean Cruising." In *Optimal Experience: Psychological Studies of Flow in Consciousness,* eds. M. Csikszentmihalyi and I. S. Csikszentmihalyi. New York: Cambridge University Press, 1988, pp. 214–31.

MacIntyre, A. *After Virtue: A Study in Moral Theory.* Notre Dame Indiana: University of Notre Dame Press, 1984.

Marniga, M. *"Dio é Morto, Nasce la Religiositá?* [God Is Dead, Is Religiosity Alive?]" *Social Trends,* 92 (2001), pp. 8–11.

Maslow, A. H. *Eupsychian Management* (reissued in 1995 as *Maslow on Management*) New York: Wiley, 1998.

———. *Towards a Psychology of Being.* New York: Van Nostrand, 1968.

———. *The Farthest Reaches of Human Nature.* New York: Viking, 1971.

Massimini, F. and A. Delle Fave. "Religion and Cultural Evolution." *Zygon,* 16:1 (1991), pp. 27–48.

Mayr, E. *The Growth of Biological Thought: Diversity, Evolution, and Inheritance.* Cambridge, Mass: Belknap Press, 1982.

Møller, V. "Happiness Trends Under Democracy: Where Will the New South African Set-Level Come to Rest?" *Journal of Happiness Studies,* 2, (2001), pp. 33–53.

Myers, D. G. *The Pursuit of Happiness: Who Is Happy—and Why.* New York: Avon, 1993.

———. "The Funds, Friends, and Faith of Happy People." *American Psychologist,* 55: 1 (2000), pp. 56–67.

Noelle-Neumann, E. *AWA Spring Survey.* Allensbach, Germany: Institut für Demoskopie Allensbach, 1995.

Novak, M. *Business as a Calling.* New York: The Free Press, 1996.

Nusbaum, H. C., and E. C. Schwab, eds. "The Role of Attention and Active Processing in Speech Perception." In *Pattern Recognition by Humans and Machines.* Vol. 1. New York: Academic Press, 1986, pp. 113–57.

O'Neil, J. R. *The Paradox of Success: When Winning at Work Means Losing at Life.* New York: Putnam, 1993.

Pardey, L. and L. Pardey. *The Self-Sufficient Sailor.* New York: Norton, 1982.

Perry, S. K. *Writing in Flow: Keys to Enhanced Creativity.* Cincinnati, Ohio: Writers' Digest Press, 1999.

Pollard, C. W. *The Soul of the Firm.* New York: HarperBusiness, 1996.

Pressner, H. B. "Can We Make Time for Children? The Economy, Work Schedules, and Child Care." *Demography,* 26:4, (1989), pp. 523–43.

Rifkin, J. *Time Wars: The Primary Conflict in Human History.* New York: Simon and Schuster, 1987.

Robinson, D. "The Climber as a Visionary." *Ascent,* 9 (1969), pp. 4–10.

Robinson, D. N. *An Intellectual History of Psychology.* Madison, Wis.: The University of Wisconsin Press, 1986.

Robinson, J. P. "The Time Squeeze." *American Demographics,* 12 (1993), pp. 12–13.

——— and G. Godbey. *Time for Life: The Surprising Ways Americans Use Their Time.* University Park, Penn.: Pennsylvania State University Press, 1997.

Rue, L. *By the Grace of Guile: The Role of Deception in Natural History and Human Affairs.* New York: Oxford University Press, 1994.

Runco, M. A., ed. *Problem-finding, Problem-solving, and Creativity.* Norwood, N. J.: Ablex, 1994.

Sahlins, M. D. *Stone Age Economics.* Chicago: Aldine Press, 1972.

Sax, L. J., A. W. Astin, W. S. Korn, and K. M. Mahoney. *The American Freshman: National Norms for Fall 1998.* Los Angeles: Higher Education Research Institute, 1998.

Schmuck, P. and K. M. Sheldon. *Life-Goals and Well-Being.* Göttingen, Germany: Hogrefe and Huber, 2001.

Schumpeter, J. *A Theory of Economic Development.* Oxford, U.K.: Oxford University Press, 1985.

Schyns, P. "Income and Satisfaction in Russia." *Journal of Happiness Studies,* 2 (2001), pp. 173–204.

Scott, M. C. *Re-Inspiring the Corporation.* Chichester, UK: John Wiley, 2000.

Seligman, M. E. P. *Authentic Happiness.* New York: Free Press, 2002.

Silver, A. D. *Entrepreneurial Megabucks.* New York: John Wiley & Sons, 1985.

Soros, G. *On Globalization.* New York: Public Affairs, 2001.

Stiglitz, J. *Globalization and Its Discontents.* New York: Norton, 2002.

Teilhard de Chardin, P. *The Phenomenon of Man.* New York: Harper and Row, 1965.

Thomas, K.W. *Intrinsic Motivation at Work: Building Energy and Commitment.* San Francisco: Berrett-Koehler, 2000.

Tolstoy, L. *Anna Karenina.* L. J. Kent and N. Berberova, eds. Translated by Constance Garnett. New York: Random House, 1993 (1878).

Vaillant, G. *Aging Well: Surprising Guideposts to a Happier Life from the Landmark Harvard Study of Adult Development.* Boston: Little, Brown, 2002.

Veenhoven, R. *Happiness in Nations.* Rotterdam, Netherlands: Erasmus University Press, 1992.

———. "Are the Russians as Unhappy as They Say They Are? Comparability of Self-Reports Across Nations." *Journal of Happiness Studies,* 2:2 (2001), pp. 111–36.

Waldrop, M. M. *Complexity: The Emerging Science at the Edge of Order and Chaos.* New York: Simon and Schuster, 1992.

Weihrouch, J. *Joy at Work.* Naperville, Ill.: JAW Publishing, 2000.

Wells, A. J. "Self-Esteem and Optimal Experience." In *Optimal Experience: Psychological Studies of Flow in Consciousness,* eds. M. Csikszentmihalyi and I.S. Csikszentmihalyi. New York: Cambridge University Press, 1988, pp. 327–41.

Wilson, D. S. *Darwin's Cathedral: Evolution, Religion, and the Nature of Society.* Chicago: The University of Chicago Press, 2002.

Wrzesniewski, A. and J. Dutton. "Crafting a Job: Revisioning Employees as Active Crafters of Their Work." *Academy of Management Review,* 26:2 (2001), pp. 179–201.

Zullow, H. M. and M. E. Seligman. "Pessimistic Rumination Predicts Defeat of Presidential Candidates, 1900 to 1984." *Psychological Inquiry, 1,*1 (1990), 52–61.

Zuzanek, J. *The Effects of Time Use and Time Pressure on Child-Parent Relationships.* Research report submitted to Health Canada. Waterloo, Ont: Otium Publications, 2000.

Index